Chambering Rifle Barrels for Accuracy

Gunsmithing Student Handbook Series

#3

By Fred Zeglin & Gordy Gritters

Chambering Rifle Barrels for Accuracy

Volume III in the Gunsmithing Student Handbook Series

Copyright© 2015, Fred Zeglin

ISBN# 978-0-9831598-5-8

Library of Congress
Control Number 2016905502

Published by
4D Reamer Rentals LTD.
432 E. Idaho St., Suite C420
Kalispell, MT 59901

Introduction

We will not only define accuracy, but look at the primary things that will affect the accuracy potential of the guns you are building.

The suggestions in this book are developed from many years of experience in full time professional gunsmithing. Maybe more important is the experience of the authors in shooting and hunting. In Part I of this book Fred Zeglin gives you an overview of what it takes to build an accurate *hunting rifle* and deals with many of the variables often overlooked or misunderstood.

Fred has been building custom hunting rifles for over thirty years. His clients come from all walks of life and have one thing in common; when they go hunting they don't want to worry about the accuracy of their rifle.

In Part II, Gordy Gritters explains the extreme accuracy requirements of a quality *benchrest* rifle. Gordy has over thirty years invested in building precision rifles. He is a competitive shooter as well as a gunsmith. Builder of many high accuracy rifles used by customers across North America to set records and win various rifle competitions including the Varmint Hunter Jamboree, Coyote Hunting National Championship, 1000 yard matches, 600 yard matches, F-Class matches, BR-50, IR 50-50, 100 and 200 yard benchrest matches, sniper matches, NRA service rifle matches, as well as for varmint and big game hunting.

If you are looking for benchrest magic, that requires lots more time and money than the techniques used for hunting rifles. At the same time, it's really just taking the same general concepts to their logical conclusion.

If you're going to do bench rest quality work then no stone should be left unturned with regard to truing the action. You as the gunsmith will spend a great deal of time dialing in, checking details and checking dimensions. Charge for this accuracy work, it has value.   FDZ

Foreword

Being a worldwide competitor and precision riflesmith offers one perks from time to time, be it components to test or to improve one's game or it may be in the form of a hunt for game to places one only dreams of. In this case, I have been honored to introduce two of my longtime friends and legends in their own fields of endeavor Fred Zeglin and Gordy Gritters to an aspect of gunsmithing that even to this day is still shrouded in a veil of mystery and dark magic, that being the "chambering" of a rifle to garner its maximum accuracy potential to make champions out of mortal men and women or take that shot of a lifetime when that trophy game presents itself to the hunter.

In these days of instant data transfer via social media, and quick DIY (Do It Yourself) videos on YouTube, that demonstrate everything from dying your poodle blue to building a Saturn V rocket, they fall short on many details of the in depth process of how to chamber a rifle barrel correctly and how to use and modify the machine tools required to do a precision job.

In this book Fred and Gordy expose the reader to everything that is necessary to accomplish a basic high quality hunting/varminting chamber job to a world class method of chambering involving documentable and measurable results through the entire process.

To the gunsmith or to the owner of a new lathe wanting to get started on the right path, Fred's knowledge of reamers and their geometry and their proper use is invaluable reading to the veteran smith and those just getting started in the field of building long range firearms. Fred establishes the foundation for precision chamber work and lathe set-up and describes all the core basics required to chamber a rifle barrel that will keep customers coming back time and time again or give one pride next time he or she takes that barrel to the range for target work or out in the field where one shot may make the difference whether we smile or cry on that long drive back home.

My friend Gordy picks up where Fred leaves off and takes the readers into the realm of super precision barrel fitting and continues to build upon what Fred has established for the readers. We now step out of Fred's "Hot Rod" and into Gordy's "Top Fuel Dragster" for those readers who are looking for the nth degree in rifle barrel accuracy hold onto your hat's boys and girls because here we go.

Gordy's skills have been tested in competition all around the world and have proved themselves in the amount of "Gold" the winners have brought home. Gordy goes on to lay out for the reader an easy to follow process for the ultimate in barrel fitting and couples each step with the theory behind each action, to provide the reader with a clear understanding as to how and why he is performing each procedure. In competition your performance is a sum of the whole, the "Perfect Firearm" married to "Perfect Performance" by the shooter to become a "Winner", with this premise in mind Gordy describes in great detail the relationship of all the rifles components to the barrel and how to create the perfect union of those components to create a rifle that could be used by national and world champions alike.

"Chambering Rifle Barrels for Accuracy" has an addition value even to the reader who will never fit a barrel to his or her own rifle. What is that you may ask? The book itself offers to the reader a contrast or comparison between different types and methods of fitting barrels to hunting, varminting, informal target shooting and the precision match rifles.

Whether you're doing your own work or having it done by someone else, the book gives you an insight as to many of the questions you may want to ask the gunsmith whom you are entrusting your rifle with to perform the work for you, this will ensure the finished product's performance meets the demands you are going to place on it and not solely on the smith to make many of the critical performance decisions for you. The reader may through the reading of Fred and Gordy's writing become aware of certain deficiencies in his or her rifle that they were never aware of and as a result have them checked or corrected to improve his or her long range performance and shooting pleasure.

I would like to take this opportunity once again to give thanks to Fred Zeglin and Gordy Gritters for being my friends for all this time and being part of this book and to introduce you the reader to a book that in my humble opinion; I feel should be the in the hands of first semester students at the gunsmithing schools around the United States. A first read to those about to delve into chambering rifle barrels of any kind and to the customers who are looking to have work done to become a more educated consumer.

Keep'em in the X-Ring,

Speedy Gonzalez

Table of Contents

Part I

Accurate Hunting Rifles
By Fred Zeglin

I have never seen an animal that was impressed by sub minute of angle (MOA) groups, have you?

The truth is that a good reliable MOA rifle will serve the needs of ninety or more percent of the shooting public. After all, MOA will allow you about a three inch group, at three-hundred yards (if you do your part). Your average elk has about a twenty-four inch heart/lung area so at normal hunting ranges there is no reason to pay the extra money for Benchrest accuracy. In the pages that follow we will lay out the basics of building a premium quality hunting rifle.

Follow is a discussion of the considerations that need to be addressed to produce a sub MOA rifle every time. While many shooters will object that they want Benchrest accuracy on all their guns, this is unrealistic. The added attention to detail that is needed to achieve Benchrest results increases the cost of the rifle by a big margin and rightly so.

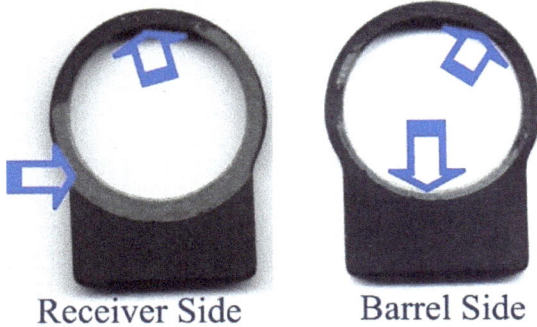

Receiver Side   Barrel Side

Above: Here is a Remington™ recoil lug as it came off a factory rifle. Note the areas where the bluing was able to penetrate and those where it was not. This is caused by uneven contact of the receiver and the barrel with the lug. Accuracy in this gun would be erratic at best. Just in case you're curious, this lug is perfectly square.

I tell all my students that if you true the action, bed the rifle correctly, do a trigger job or replace the trigger with a top quality unit and the ammo is well made you will get 90% of the benefits that come from a Benchrest barrel job, maybe more?

Action tuning (blueprinting or truing) is the process of making all the parts that make up the action square and true to the bore. First the locking lugs of the bolt must be lapped to insure even solid contact with the locking surfaces in the receiver. When finished the lugs should have equal contact area and contact should exceed 80%. This is accomplished using lapping compounds which produce smooth even surfaces. Be sure to use a non-embedding compound, clean all the lapping compound out of the locking recesses when you're finished to prevent continued wear.

The next step is to face the receiver square to the axis of the bore. We see this on nearly every brand of action, although it does vary in degree. Naturally, custom actions are often much better with regard to these problems as they are not mass produced and you are paying for the special attention to detail.

To face the action, a precision mandrel is inserted into the action to hold it true to the axis of the bore. The mandrel and action are then placed on the lathe and a small amount of material is cut off the front of the receiver where it will contact the shoulder of the barrel. Only enough material is removed to square up the front of the receiver, so no strength is lost.

Remove the mandrel. Then we insert the bolt in the action and measure from the receiver face down to the bolt face. A standard for the bolt face of plus or minus .0005 inches across the face will produce a high degree of accuracy. If this standard is held along with the facing of the receiver and the lapping of the lugs, sub minute of angle groups will result. In cases where the bolt face does not meet this specification use a mandrel and a steady rest to hold the bolt in a lathe to cut the bolt face square.

Note that I did not suggest rethreading the action to improve accuracy. The reason I did not is that about 90% of the accuracy potential of any bolt action can be realized simply by making sure the receiver and bolt face are squared and perpendicular to the bore of the barrel and the lugs are lapped as above.

Barrel Lapping. Lapping the bore can offer more uniformity and therefore accuracy. This process removes the small burrs and marks left in the bore from the machine process. It also polishes the bore, which reduces fouling. A side benefit is that, there is little or no "break in" for a lapped bore, which saves lots of time, money, and tedious cleaning. Some top match barrels are lapped from the factory, Hart and Lilja are two examples.

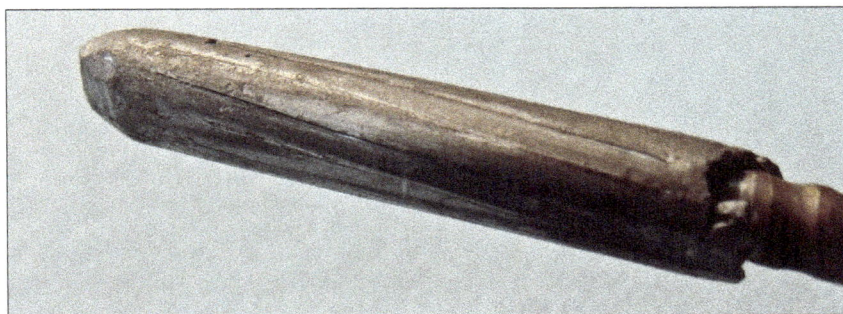

Cast lead barrel lap. This is the method often used by gunsmiths to remove imperfections and uniform the bore. The lap is on a brass rod with a T handle that allows the rod to spin with the turn of the rifling. Non-imbedding lapping compound is used to lap the bore.

Normally this process is only offered on barrels that are not yet fit to a gun, i.e. blank barrels. The reason for this is the need to clean up the area where the brass rod tends to rub as it enters the bore. If you are working with a blank it is easy to allow the act of chambering to cut away any damage to the rifling. It is possible to lap a finished barrel but great care must be taken not to damage the throat or the muzzle.

Lap from the breech end of the barrel. Do not allow the lap to exit fully out the muzzle as it will become misaligned with the rifling. I install a stop on the rod so that the lap cannot exit the muzzle.

Mark the rod and barrel so that if you take the lap out of the bore you can align it back with the same rifling grooves. Inserting the lap in the wrong grooves in many cases will prove to be detrimental to the bore, no two grooves are identical in form.

Lapping from some barrel makers is not performed in this manner. Many makers use a tight fitting brush with a man-made sapphire lapping compound. The stones are tiny, about 30 microns. This process is much easier than lead lapping but is more of a polishing operation than a dimension uniforming process.

Barrel fit is the next consideration. The barrel must be set up on the lathe so that it is centered perfectly on the bore. Centering the barrel on the bore insures that it will be mounted squarely in the action. The shoulder will be exactly 90 degrees to the bore and the threads will be concentric to the bore, all essential to accuracy.

Crown is equally as important for accuracy as any other aspect of the job. It also must be concentric to give best accuracy. Over the years I have tried many styles of crowns at many different angles to the bore. Some work better than others but the bottom line is always the same, if it is concentric it will be accurate.

An 11 degree target crown will normally produce the best accuracy from any given barrel. Be sure not to leave any burrs standing up on the crown, this can cause deflection of the bullet base as it leaves the bore of the barrel (accuracy will suffer).

Such burrs can be eliminated by either lapping the muzzle with a brass lap and some very fine valve grinding compound. Another method commonly used is a 45 degree muzzle cutter, these cutters are piloted and are used to gently hand cut the burr away at the muzzle, but not as a crown. The idea is to put a tiny bevel on the ends of the lands and just deburr the bottom of the groove.

Cryo Treatment can improve accuracy. Over many years of experience I have seen a reduction in group size of from 30 to 50%, where the barrels were tested before and after. Chromoly barrels (blue steel) benefit from cryo stress relief.

Metallurgists will tell you that stainless does not benefit from cryo treatment, so don't waste the money on stainless. The reason for this has to do with the grain structure of stainless vs. chromoly and the fact that the temperature ranges used do not affect the temper of stainless steel.

Trigger jobs can do more for accuracy than you might think. These days the factories are shipping guns with trigger pulls of five to eight pounds. To add insult to injury they include lots of sear engagement (shooters call that 'Creep'). Winchester and Remington triggers can be stoned and adjusted to good hunting weights of 3 lbs.

Most novice or hunter class gun owners will find a well-tuned 3 lb. pull to be very light. The control over the moment of ignition that a crisp trigger provides is much of what a hunter needs to get sub MOA group on a consistent basis.

There are aftermarket triggers available for most actions these days. Pull weights with these triggers vary according to the manufacturer and or model chosen. Utilizing one of these triggers designed for a pull lighter than 3 lbs. is the only reliable way to avoid liability for a light trigger.

A sales representative for one large manufacturer told me that he had executives in a production meeting ask why they should be concerned with triggers lighter than five pounds. He politely explained that if they had to ask that question they needed to visit several web sites. He then listed all the aftermarket trigger makers he could think of. Pointing to the list he said, "These guys are making a good living replacing crappy factory triggers."

Pull weights lighter than 3 lbs. require an experienced shooter to be safe. Group size can be greatly reduced by a good trigger, just ask a bench rest shooter. Although aftermarket triggers can be set to weights below 3 lbs., this can present liability concerns. Use your own best judgment concerning such triggers.

Bedding varies a little from one action to the next. The best method on average is to free float the barrel and bed the action.

H-S Precision Inc. originated the milled aluminum bedding block in their line of synthetic stocks. The bedding block is much like a V block and takes care of bedding, some tuning can make the aluminum bedding system even more accurate. Many other stock makers now offer similar systems.

If you think of the bedding block as a V block and simply scrape away any contact areas that would deflect from that V arrangement, accuracy can be maximized with this bedding system. I would normally only place bedding compound behind the recoil lug to insure even/solid contact with this type of bedding block. The rest is metal on metal.

Other options for bedding stocks are pillar bedding and glass bedding. Pillars are made from metal usually aluminum, the purpose is to add a support to the stock so that it cannot be crushed by the action screws. The pillars also add stability to the bedding job.

At Left: Adjustable pillar kit from Score High Gunsmithing for the Remington 700. Also available for Winchester 70/ Montana 1999 and Howa 1500/ Weatherby Vanguard.

You can of course buy or fabricate generic pillars that can be fit to most any bolt action. All you need is some aluminum and a lathe.

Glass bedding is the most common method used to accurize stocks. Fiberglass and epoxy are used to bed the action of the rifle. This

18

adds stability and protection from humidity. Proper bedding requires an understanding of the pressure points of the action and the methods that will provide the best support and results. A good bedding job will improve accuracy and help make the rifle less susceptible to temperature and humidity changes.

See our Bedding Hunting Rifles booklet in the Gunsmithing Student Handbook Series for greater detail.

Quality ammunition is a product of good reloading skills and tools. There are many makers of reloading dies. Quality varies widely from one manufacturer to the next. All will work to produce usable ammunition. Accurate ammo requires better quality dies. Just like the rifle, the dies must be concentric in order to be accurate.

Think of it this way, if you were to draw a 12 inch long line on a piece of paper with a ruler held firmly down you will get a single clean line from end to end. What happens if you stop every inch and pick the ruler up, replace it on the paper, and continue the line? Likely no matter how careful you are the line will not be perfectly straight. When we reload ammo we are picking up the ruler with every component used and with every process executed.

Each component must be as concentric and accurately made as possible. This is why you often hear top competitors in shooting events talk of using brass from 'one lot,' it provides uniformity. Primer pockets must be the same depth from case to case. The primer must be seated to the same depth on each case. The cases must not be bent, some dies will actually bend the neck of the case. Powder charges must be carefully weighed so that each charge is the same as the last. (There is a school of thought that prefers to just accept the volume dropped by the powder measure for accuracy). Both methods work well and their individual proponents will defend them almost to the death.

Good quality bullets must be used, if they are cheap there is usually a reason. Care must be taken when seating bullets not to bend the case in the die. Conventional bullet seaters will often bend the neck because the bullet is not held concentric during the seating process. Inline bullet seaters will solve this problem. The idea is to hold the case and the bullet directly in line while seating the bullet.

The last consideration is seating depth, here again uniformity is the name of the game. Seating depth is established best by using one of the commercial devices available on the market for this purpose.

Once the seating depth is established start by seating your bullet .050 inches off the lands. Do some shooting to find your most accurate powder and charge. Once you have located a good load varying the seating depth will help tighten the groups. Start by seating the bullet deeper by an additional .010 inches at a time. Fire test groups, when you find the best group sometimes adjusting the seating depth by .005 inches one way or the other will tighten the group even further. Best accuracy usually occurs between .050 and .080 inches of jump; we are talking about hunting here so the safety provided by that jump is extremely valuable. Contrary to popular opinion, only on rare occasion does seating the bullet closer to the lands produce more accurate results. If you seat closer than .050" to the lands remember that is a set up best used only when punching paper, not out in the field where all kinds of variables and dirt can get into the mix.

I often hear shooters talk about seating out the bullet to touch the lands of the barrel. Benchrest shooters get away with this practice because they are normally loading below peak pressures. Or at the very least, conditions for bench rest shooting allow the shooter to spot problems that a hunter could easily miss in the field.

Seating to the lands is OK for forming brass but is dangerous in hunting situations, as bullets can stick in the throat when extracting live rounds. Also pressure spikes can occur if the bullet is touching the lands. Testing has proven over and over that a bullet seated touching the throat can raise peak pressure by as much as 8000 PSI, (about 13% for an average full pressure high intensity load) that is substantial!

Better consistency and therefore accuracy will come from bullets seated away from the rifling lands. In a hunting rifle, never seat any closer to the lands than you must to achieve accuracy.

Setting up to Install the Barrel

Many gunsmiths and hobbyists have simply used a four jaw chuck and a spider on the headstock of the lathe to dial both ends of the bore in. The problem with this method is that no barrel is drilled totally straight through the blank. However, this method will deliver MOA or better accuracy, nearly every time.

Range Rods are popular these days to dial in the bore of the barrel. There are several variations on these tools, all will work. Choice of tools has more to do with your working methods and experience than the specific tools. Picture below is one style. The pilot from the reamer is used on the range rod to dial in the bore of the barrel. The idea is to insure that the bore is straight for the length of the bore that the reamer will be working in.

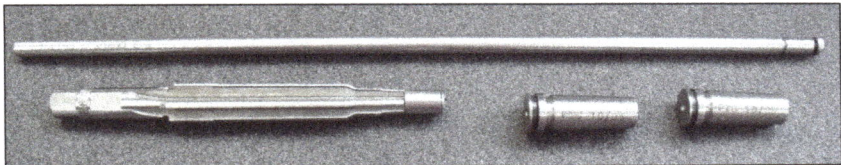

Above is a Grizzly range rod (designed by Gordy Gritters) along with reamer and gauges for a magnum chamber. The rod is straight in real life, just an illusion caused by the camera lens.

No barrel is perfectly straight, so the range rod allows you to align the bore by dialing the breech in a four jaw chuck and then dialing in the muzzle end of the barrel utilizing an outboard spider.

You can use aluminum shims on about a quarter inch at the tip of the chuck jaws to protect the barrel and to allow the barrel to pivot a little when the spider is adjusted to align the bore. Any longer than that often prevents the barrel from camming as we desire here.

21

In the case of range rods we are dialing in the length of the chamber, not the entire barrel. The idea being that if the bore is aligned to the lathe then a more accurate chamber will result.

It is best to thread the barrel once it is dialed in rather than between centers. This insures the barrel threads are aligned to the bore.

If you choose to thread the barrel between centers or you must due to the configuration of the barrel, then make sure the barrel is centered properly on the bore.

60 degree center cutter at left uses a pilot make sure the bevel on the end of the barrel blank is concentric to the bore. Photo courtesy of PTG.

If working between centers I do a little extra truing of the barrel diameter. Sporter tapers normally have a straight cylindrical area at the breech with no taper. Taking a skim cut on the cylindrical area will make it very close to concentric to the bore. This makes it heat more evenly in use and removes just one more alibi from the mechanics of the barrel.

Thread the barrel and fit it to the action so that you can set the headspace to match the action. Of course the Savage barrel pictured below has adjustable headspace via the factory barrel nut.

But most barrels require the headspace to be set specific to the action you are using.

Trial fit the action to the barrel to make sure the action shoulders up solid and the bolt can be installed and closes without interference.

Obviously there are numerous different breeching methods specific to the design of the action. It is wise to always leave .005" to .010" space between the bolt surfaces and the back of the barrel. If the bolt is allowed to contact the barrel it will cause accuracy problems. When the bolt touches the barrel it creates a teetering point so the bolt never settles in the same location for a string of shots.

In addition to the need to keep the bolt from touching the barrel the prescribed clearance also allows for dirt, grime, brass particles and unburned powder to have room to escape. These items will cause accuracy and reliability issues if the breech is fit too tight.

With the barrel fit to the action now we are ready to actually chamber the barrel. It should go without saying that the action is again removed following the trial fit of the action.

In the next chapter we will discuss in detail the advantages and disadvantages of removable pilots and fixed pilots. For the sake of simplicity let's just state that the pilot should be between .0005" and .001" under the bore diameter. Bore diameter being the distance across the lands of the barrel. This is best determined with pin gauges. Nearly all chatter in chambers can be traced to improper fit of the pilot to the bore.

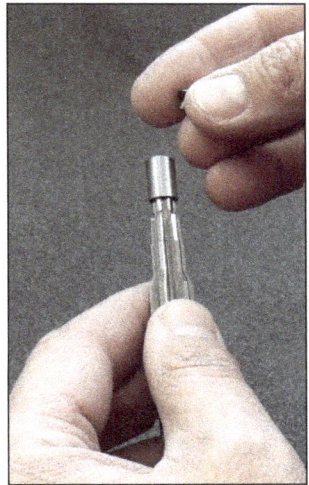

There are numerous ways to hold the reamer during the reaming process. No matter how well you dial in your lathe and tail stock there is always a chance they will be out of alignment some way.

For this reason the use of a floating reamer holder is an easy way to insure the reamer will stay aligned to the bore.

There are a number of floating reamer holders on the market. Shown at right is a Clymer reamer holder. Reamer holders vary in the way they handle the reamer. Some allow only movement along the axis of the bore. Others allow movement perpendicular to the bore as well.

If your machine is in good condition and the tail stock is properly aligned to the bore of the lathe then only axial movement is required for top quality results.

Micrometer Reamer Stops

Simple stops have been made and used by gunsmiths for as long as there have been reamers. The simple stops are just a donut or collar normally made of steel with a set screw. The stop is slid over the reamer and positioned so it will stop the reamer against the back of the barrel. If you wanted "micrometer" adjustment, simply put a similar collar on the shank of the reamer so you can measure between the stops and make adjustments by moving the stop that touches the barrel.

The value of course to an adjustable reamer stop is the ability to quickly hone in on the headspace you need. While the beginner will enjoy the ease with which they are able to set headspace, the professional will love the time they save chambering using a reamer stop. Even more important there will be far fewer mistakes in the depth of the chamber, again saving time. They can be utilized for repeatability, either in production or in matching one chamber to another. Probably most important is the ability to precisely set the length of throats with ease.

Someone is always working on a better mouse trap, so there are two commercial micrometer reamer stops on the market today. One is from a gunsmith and inventor named Nat Lambeth his company is called Custom Guns and Ammunition, LLC. His design, called the MARS II, utilizes several different size collars so you can use it on almost any reamer you have.

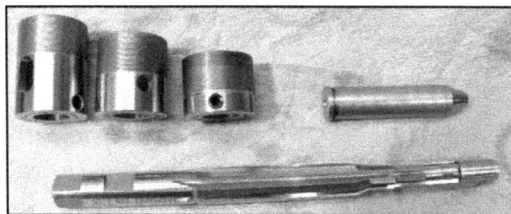

Lambeth Reamer stop Collars come in several lengths to work with any reamer length.

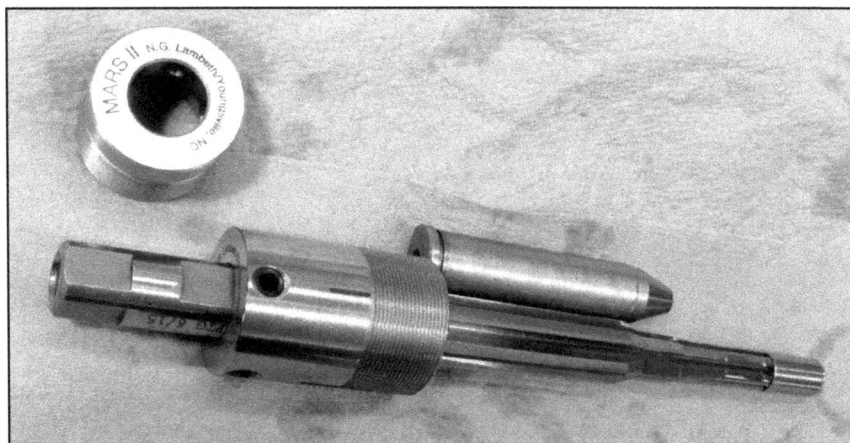

To set up the MARS II you simply select the correct length collar to install on the reamer. A headspace gauge or piece of brass for the chamber to be reamed can be used to estimate the correct length and locate the MARS II on the shank. You purposely position it so that the chamber will be about 1/16" shallow or a little more. This allows the final measurements to be made directly on your barrel and action.

25

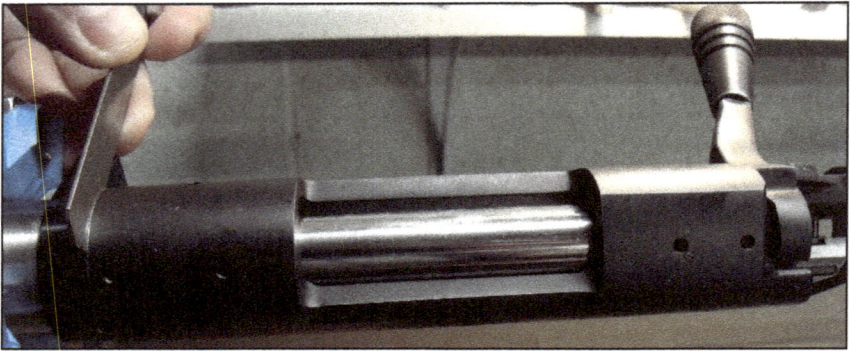

When you get to that last little bit. Clean the chamber and use the headspace gauge as shown here. The firing pin and ejector are removed. Gently thread the action into place, close the bolt on the headspace gauge and when the receiver will not go any further (light touch) use a feeler gauge to measure just how far you have to go.

The final step is to adjust the reamer stop to the desired headspace measurement.

Adjusting the MARS II reamer stop in the picture above. Here you can see the number and indication line. Since it's adjustable in 1/1000 of an inch, you can easily dial right to your finished dimensions. Lambeth provides very complete instructions on the use of his tool.

Reamer stops like this are designed for use on manual machines where you have the ability to feel when the stop comes in contact with the back of the barrel. They would not be used on a CNC setup.

P.O. Ackley Reamer Stop

Another model that is on the market is named the P.O. Ackley Micrometer Reamer Stop. Truth is there is no evidence that Ackley ever made a reamer stop like this. Likely it was simply named for him. This particular stop is manufactured by Pacific Tool & Gauge and is simpler in design to the Lambeth tool. Simplicity might mean that it works with fewer tools, but it also means it's a little easier to use. All of the stops described here can be used in conjunction with a floating reamer holder.

The Ackley stop is simpler in construction with fewer pieces but in truth the MARS II stop because of its wide range of length setups will work with nearly any caliber of reamer. There is something to be said for having all that potential for variation ready and at hand. If I had to pick… Probably more options will sway my decision.

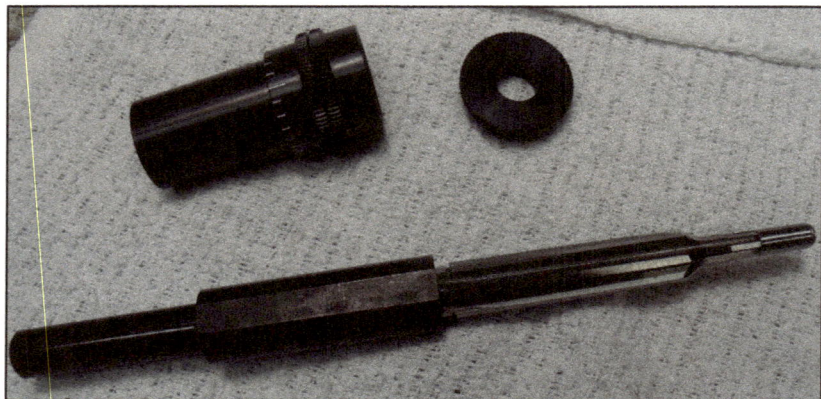

The Ackley Reamer Stop includes the reamer holder pictured at the bottom of this photo. The Stop parts pictured above slip onto the holder and rough length is set with a pair of set screws. Fine adjustments are done with the two stop collars, the indicator marks allow for .001" adjustment.

Above is the assembled stop. The forward most collar would stop against the back of the barrel to stop the reamer from cutting further and set headspace.

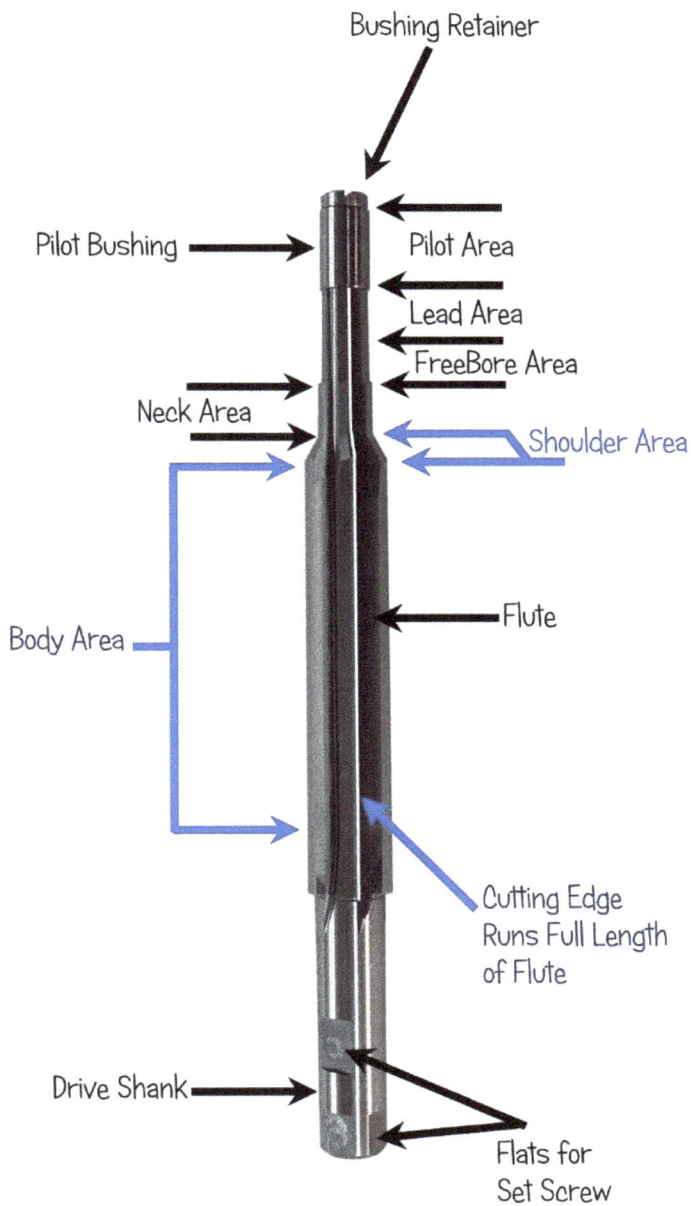

Bushing Retainer

Pilot Bushing

Pilot Area

Lead Area

FreeBore Area

Neck Area

Shoulder Area

Body Area

Flute

Cutting Edge
Runs Full Length
of Flute

Drive Shank

Flats for
Set Screw

Reamer Nomenclature

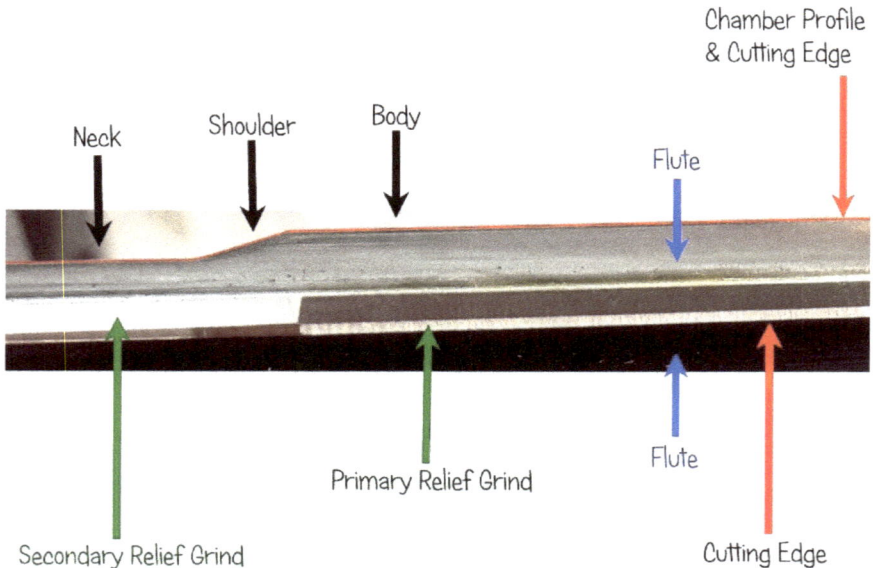

Neck · Shoulder · Body · Chamber Profile & Cutting Edge · Flute · Primary Relief Grind · Secondary Relief Grind · Flute · Cutting Edge

Note that in the above picture, the grinds and cutting edges run the full length of each flute. In this picture you have one cutting edge outlined in red facing up. Another cutting edge is pointed at you. Flutes here are identified as the chip relief part of the reamer.

Now it's time to start reaming.

If you're in a production shop where you are performing multiple chamberings of the same cartridge then a roughing reamer is a good idea. By roughing the chamber, wear is saved on the finish reamer. It's not at all essential that you rough the chamber first. You can chamber fully with just the finish reamer. It simply takes more time.

I will commit gunsmithing heresy here by saying that you can use a drill bit to rough a chamber. Be sure to leave about .030" or more material for the finish reamer to clean up (.015" per side). In order to get away with the drill bit roughing, it is essential that you keep the reamer pilot engaged in the bore. Measure the length of the pilot, neck and shoulder, always stop drilling soon enough to leave at least .050" of the pilot engaged in the bore when the reamer begins to cut.

This engagement of the pilot is necessary to prevent damage to the reamer and to prevent chatter. If the pilot is not in the bore the reamer will be able to dig into the chamber wall and will either be broken or the chamber will end up gouged out oversized.

If you're trying to accomplish benchrest accuracy I would not rough the chamber. If you do, it would be wise to go in with a boring bar to clean up any error the roughing may have introduced. In order to use the boring bar you will want to leave more material in the chamber area to clean up. Leave at least .020" to .030" per side so you will have enough material to easily bring things back on center.

Dave Kiff of Pacific Tool & Gauge recommends petroleum base high sulfur cutting fluid such as, TRIM OM 300, Castrol ILOCUT 534, Texaco Transultex H, Chevron Lanka Cutting Oil, and Mobile met Alpha Cutting Oil. All of these can be cut with a 20% ATF Transmission Fluid for better finish with 4140 Military Steel.

Other cutting fluids that work are Vipers Venom, Spectrum® Cutting Oil or Tap Magic™. Tap Magic is not the best choice but works in a pinch, as Kiff recommends, I would choose a Sulfur based oil as well whenever possible.

Rechambering Existing Barrels

Rechamber jobs by their very nature require that you either set the barrel back one thread and rechamber to the same cartridge, or you must chamber to a larger/longer cartridge to clean up the old chamber completely.

It's a pretty simple matter to check chamber dimensions to insure the new cartridge will work in the old barrel.

1. Check the length of the new cartridge against the original chamber. It must be longer to clean up the old chamber.

31

2. Check the shoulder diameter; it should be larger than the original chamber.
3. Check the junction of the shoulder and the body, it must be forward of the old location of the start of the shoulder.
4. Check the junction of the shoulder and the neck, it must be forward of the old location of the same junction.

In short the new case must be big enough to clean up the old chamber. This can be assisted by the act of setting the barrel back one or two turns as needed.

Barrel Setback is the task of machining the shoulder of the barrel back so that the barrel can turn further into the receiver. This process can be used to correct excessive headspace, to regain a little life if the throat of the barrel is eroded and to insure a new chamber will be totally devoid of any remnants of the original.

Depending upon the action in question the process may vary a little, but the bottom line is a barrel setback simply moves the chamber forward by shortening the breech. Normally, only one thread is used, this allows sights and barrel markings to return to the proper clocked positions. It is also possible to go a half turn to bury old markings under the wood line if no sights need to be clocked.

Customers sometimes worry that this will cause gaps in the bedding around the barrel. It's not a problem as the barrel is normally moved back about $1/16^{th}$ of an inch. Consequently, in most cases the customer can't even tell the difference.

To be clear, material is machined off the shoulder of the barrel where it touches the receiver and an equal amount is normally taken off the back of the barrel too, so that the bolt will not contact the barrel. If you're working with a rimmed cartridge as in many lever guns, then you must take into account the headspace, as the rim rests on the back of the barrel and with levers we are often tightening headspace when performing a setback.

Dealing with Extractors

When rechambering a barrel with an extractor slot it is necessary to deal with an interrupted cut. Many a chamber reamer has been damaged or broken when a novice gunsmith tried to rechamber a barrel with an extractor or ejector cut.

At left is the breech end of a New England Firearms® (NEF) barrel that is about to be rechambered. The mistake that is commonly made is to try to insert the chamber reamer into this existing chamber without preparing the chamber area. Reamers are not made to work on an interrupted cut such as an extractor cut. Trying to use a conventional drill bit will not work in this situation either; it will simply do a lot of damage and make a mess of the job.

There are two easy ways to handle this problem and end up with a nice clean chamber.

1. Use a piloted counter bore to cut a recess that will accept the chamber reamer, eliminating the extractor cut. The problem with this method is that you would need a specialty tool for every chamber diameter that you might decide to rechamber for.

2. Place the barrel in the lathe and use a boring bar or a simple boring tool hand ground for the purpose. This method has the advantage of working on any cartridge combination that you might encounter.

Bore out the area of the extractor cut to a dimension very close that of the shoulder diameter of the reamer you will be using. The idea again is to prevent the reamer from cutting an interrupted cut. As the shoulder of the reamer engages the chamber it will then cut uniformly and without chatter.

If you attempt to cut the chamber without performing this preparation, each flute of the reamer will bang against the interrupted cut as it comes around. In most cases this will at a minimum damage the reamer, worst case it will break the reamer.

At right is a simple hand ground lathe bit that will work for this job. The underside of the tool must be relieved so that it can clearance the inside of the chamber area. This is a finesse job, only remove as much as you need to get the reamer in full contact with the barrel.

Here is the chamber area after the boring work is done and before the reamer has been used. Note that we did not cut away any unnecessary material, only that which will make the reamer cut properly. Chatter is a common complaint when rechambering a barrel. The pilot is often either not engaged in the bore of

the barrel or it does not fit the barrel properly. Trying to chamber without the pilot being engaged at least .100" is just asking for chatter. If there is no way to keep the pilot engaged, then run the machine as slow as possible, and feed the tool slowly allowing it to cut without stress.

A simple way to stop chatter that will not damage the tool is to wrap the reamer with a strip of wax paper. The wax paper acts as a dampener against the chatter which is caused by vibration. Use cutting oil as normal when using the wax paper. All you need is a strip about .500" wide and long enough to wrap the reamer about three times around. You will have to hold the wax paper in place as the reamer enters the chamber, once in the chamber the reamer will trap the wax paper, ream as normal.

The chamber below completely cleaned up the old rim cut from the rimmed cartridge. Of course the extractor would have to be modified for the rimless case.

Side note: Reamers for straight wall cases like black powder and pistol type cartridges are prone to damage from the problems addressed above. A little attention to detail will save you any problems.

In addition they are prone to damage near the rim cutter when chips become trapped in the extractor cut. So, if you're working with such reamers take extra care to keep chips cleared, especially when nearing the last few cuts.

Tolerance Stacking, Everything You Need to Know About Pilots.

Chamber reamers come with two styles of pilots, solid or removable bushing (the later sometimes called a floating pilot). One is evil and one is practically perfection. But which is which? I can tell you that in renting tools to gunsmiths I have found the industry is split on this question about 50/50. In other words, about half demand solid pilot reamers exclusively and the other half will not touch those nasty solid pilots with a ten foot pole.

It is clear that there is a trend toward the removable pilot reamers. This is because barrel makers are not all holding to the same production standards. Some have the idea that a tighter bore is better, while other makers hold close to the "standard" bore dimensions. Example, .308 bores are .300" on the bore and .308" on the groove. Custom barrel makers have tightened the bore to say .298" This will required a smaller pilot as the standard pilots are normally .299" with tolerances of + 0 to - .0005".

At right: Removable (floating) pilot reamer.

The reason for the tighter bore? In short, it is believed that it produces better accuracy. This is only true as compared to a loose bore that is oversized, i.e. a groove on a 30 caliber of .309 or .310 will produce lower pressures and potentially be less accurate because the bullet is not fully engaged until pressure bumps the bullet up to match the bore.

For a pilot to work correctly it should be .001" smaller than the actual bore dimension. In other words, it needs to be a close slip fit. If a pilot is too tight it will bind and likely break the reamer, and possibly damage the bore. If a pilot is too loose it will promote chatter. It is possible to run the pilot on a removable pilot reamer closer to the bore diameter (.0005" under bore diameter is ideal), but it must still slip easily in and out to avoid damage to the barrel or the tools.

A little history at this point might be interesting: Red Elliot was and still is legendary with old timer gunsmiths as the absolute best reamer maker of the last century. Near as I can tell he was the first to offer removable pilots on his reamers. Why did he do this? Well, he found that there were enough different barrel makers in his day that the dimensions of the bore diameter (where the pilot rides) varied a fair amount.

So, this problem of bore dimensions changing a little is nothing new. What about SAAMI standards you say? I will address that in just a moment, for now let's talk about how Red Elliot handled bushing pilots.

I have seen several of Red's reamers with bushing type pilots, what we sometimes call floating pilots today. Red held very tight tolerances on his bushings so that it required a little pressure to slide them onto the reamer, held in place by a screw mounted in the end of the reamer the bushing would not turn once the screw was tightened. This is contrary to the bushing pilots we see commonly used today, where the bushing is a slip fit with about .0005" tolerance internally. This tolerance is added for manufacturing ease. Tolerance stacking is not usually mentioned in conjunction with floating pilot reamers, but we are going to take a closer look at it here.

Another source of tolerance issues is the fact that the pilot receiver on the reamer must be concentric (round), and in line with the reamer. If either of these conditions is not correct there will be problems with the reamer cutting oversized or out of alignment with the bore. Admittedly, this is not much of an issue with today's cnc machines. So long as the operator does not make an error, and no chips get caught in the set-up. One other possible source of trouble would be a warped reamer (not common).

Now for SAAMI, their standards are voluntary, so obviously any barrel maker can decide whether or not to hold solid to the standards. Industry standard is plus or minus a half thousandth (+ or − 0.0005") on the bore diameter. The bore diameter is the smallest diameter of the barrel, also referred to by shooters as "across the lands". The same tolerance applies to the groove of the barrel. I will leave the discussion of groove depth as we are talking about bore diameter as it relates to chambering tools, groove depth does not affect these dimensions.

Admittedly barrels considered "match" grade or "air gaged" are supposed to be held to a tolerance of .0003" or less total variance, end to end of the barrel. This does not indicate the actual bore diameter, we are left to assume that it is the standard diameter for caliber. In the case of a 30 calibers we would be talking about a .300" bore. What if the maker decides to simply use a gage that works with the bore diameter they are making, say .2995" and it air gages as above. You have a match grade barrel but the bore is at the minimum size according to industry standards.

Are you starting to see how bores can vary and still be within standards?

Of course there are those makers who operate outside the standards and make perfectly good barrels. The point being; different size pilots will be needed to chamber these barrels as was recognized back in the 1950's and 60's by Red Elliot. It's pretty obvious by now that removable pilots are necessary tools in dealing with variations in bore dimensions. It should be clear by now that variations in bore diameter of plus or minus .001" or even more, is not that unusual, even though such dimensions may or may not follow the voluntary standards set by SAAMI.

Solid pilot reamers offer certain advantages over the floating pilot. First and most obvious there is no built in tolerance between the bushing and the reamer, because there is no bushing.

At right: Solid Pilot Reamer

Since most barrel makers today are making barrels by the button rifled method, dimensions tend to remain pretty steady for a given maker as buttons last a long time if properly cared for. So if you deal with the same barrel maker all the time chances are a solid pilot reamer will fit the same from barrel to barrel.

There are other factors that play into the bore and groove dimensions, but that is a discussion for another book.

One limitation of a solid pilot reamer is that it cannot be changed to deal with variations in bore diameters. Of course you can have the pilot ground down if necessary to fit a tight bore, but then you would probably need a second or even a third reamer to deal with various diameter bores.

Everything in life is a trade-off. Because of the expense of multiple reamers for the same caliber removable pilots are a cost effective answer to the problem. $10 for a bushing beats $100 or more for another reamer. There are shops that stock bushings in 0.0002" steps for the popular calibers. This allows them to match the bushing to the bore every time.

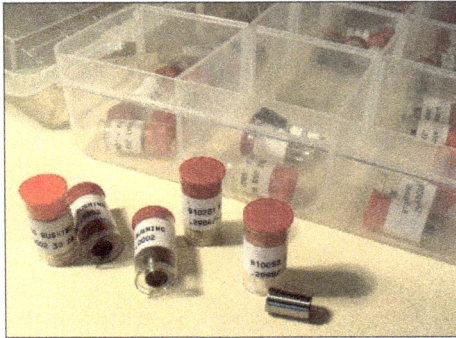

Pilot bushings can be a big investment. Speedy Gonzalez, world class Bench Rest gunsmith says he orders a different diameter pilot with each reamer he orders. So if you are ordering 30 caliber reamers order a different pilot diameter on each to save on the cost of collecting pilots.

To make the use of removable pilots efficient and accurate, the gunsmith should invest in a set of pin gauges. These are precision ground pins that can be used to gauge the bore and insure that the correct bushing is selected. Using pin gauges allows the gunsmith to know what bore diameter the barrel maker is really supplying.

Now keep in mind the pilot has to slip into the bore, so in mechanical terms the pilot has to be about 0.0004" smaller than the bore to slip in without any interference. In most shops the pilot is figured at 0.001" smaller than the bore and rightly so. Too tight a fit can gall and or leave marks in the bore or stress the reamer and break it during the reaming process.

What happens if the pilot is too loose?

Ninety-Nine times out of a hundred when a reamer chatters (vibrates) in use, it is because the pilot to bore fit is too loose.

The lack of support when the pilot is too small allows the reamer to move around in the bore, as the tool tries to bite into the steel it grabs hard and because even tool steel is flexible you get chatter as the tool loads and releases tension. This is the reason that some gunsmith's insist on having a set of pilots that cover the possible variations in .0002" (That's 2/10,000 of an inch.) increments. Keeping the pilot as close to bore dimensions as possible will help eliminate chatter and promote a more precise chamber.

If you have a pilot that is a perfect match for the bore but is too loose on the inside where it rides on the reamer then the advantage of a close fitting pilot is negated. To pull the whole concept together... If you have a .0002" tolerance on your bushing to barrel fit and the same on the pilot to reamer fit, you end up with .0004" total slop on the pilot.

I can tell you that most people do not grasp this or understand why these tolerances matter. I base that statement on 30 years of talking to gunsmithing customers, and the people who call to rent tools. The comments that shooters and gunsmiths make during our conversations indicate their level of understanding in a hurry.

In general if the total pilot run-out is under .001" then all will work fine and there should be no worries. This rule holds true for solid pilot or removable pilot reamers. Long ago I lost track of how many rechamber and barrel jobs I have done. I can tell you that it is possible to get an accurate job from either type of reamer. In fact, if pressed for a choice I would say that solid pilot reamers are more accurate on average. Especially for inexperienced gunsmiths.

I do not make this statement lightly, as I own hundreds of reamers of both types. This goes back to the understanding of how the tools relate to the barrel. To reiterate, the one caveat would be that for best accuracy the pilot of the reamer must meet the tolerances of less than .001" run out verses the bore, for all this to hold true.

There is another major factor in how well a reamer cuts and how accurate the gun will be… The gunsmith must do a good job on the set up for machining. If the threads are not true to the bore, or the chamber is crooked or oversized, or the throat of the chamber ends up off center, accuracy will be elusive to say the least.

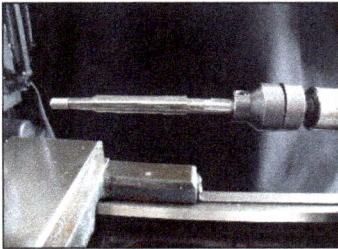

Use of a floating reamer holder is a great way to insure an accurate chamber. This tool allows the reamer to follow the hole in the barrel without any side pressure that might be caused by minor misalignment of the tail stock to the bore of the lathe.

Other Considerations with Reamers.

Chamber reamers are pretty complex tools that incorporate all the features of the chamber into one form cutting tool.

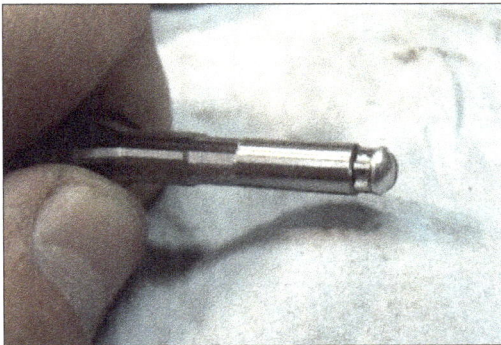

Above is pictured the tip of a chamber reamer. You can see from left to right the shoulder, neck, throat, and pilot.

41

Note that the pilot pictured above appears to be short for the reamer. It was not short when the pilot bushing was new. A novice used this tool, the bushing was too tight a fit for the bore. Proper fit is .0005" to .001" under the bore diameter. That makes for a nice slip fit of the bushing to the bore of the barrel. The pilot bushing rides on the lands (bore) of the barrel.

How do I know the bushing was too tight for the bore?

Simple, the bushing was forced back onto the cutting edge hard enough that the throat actually cut the back of the pilot. Note in the picture at left, the same bushing off the reamer. You can see where the tool cut the bushing. This portion of the reamer is not very sharp as it was never intended to cut anything. So that is how I know this bushing was forced into a tight bore.

The primary reason for using removable pilot bushings is so that you can match the pilot to the bore of your barrel. No need to force things.

You know this guy has no idea how a reamer works...

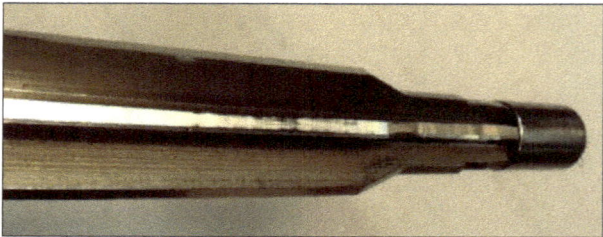

The reamer above was "sharpened" by a "gunsmith". The large flat running down the center of the picture has two grinds. The fat grind closer to the top of the picture is a secondary relief grind, meaning it will never touch the barrel, it is clearance ground to make sure that chips will not get caught behind the cutting edge.

The narrow grind just below the relief grind is where the actual cutting edge is located. This grind is also relief ground just slightly, this is the primary relief grind. Only the very edge where the grind meets the flute is actually touching the barrel during chambering. So in the picture the cutting edge is facing down.

If you stone on the outside grinds of the reamer the dimensions change very quickly because the geometry of the cutting edge and the clearance grind. Never stone on the outside edge unless you have been trained to do so.

If you look inside the flute on top of the cutting edge where the chips gather during cutting that is the area that you can stone without changing the dimensions of the reamer. In the picture on page 44 that would be the surface facing you on the bottom flute where the chip is welded.

Again, because of the geometry of the reamer; stoning on this inside edge changes dimensions such a tiny amount that it should not create any problems with chamber size if you don't get carried away. Normally all that is needed is the cleaning of metal built up on the cutting edge, little or no real stoning of the reamer itself.

When looking at the picture of the reamer above, I laugh, because you can see where the "gunsmith" stoned on the relief grind. Since this part of the reamer never touches the barrel at any time it is clear that this guy had no idea how the tool works. If you don't know how a tool works, it's a safe bet you have no business trying to sharpen it. Send it to the reamer maker if you're not sure, it's cheaper than an angry customer and an out of spec chamber.

Metal build up on reamers.

Such build-up is often mistaken for damage or dullness of the reamer. It is caused by several things. Most prominent causes would be little or no lubrication when cutting, poor quality lubrication, pushing the tool too fast and/or too hard. Other less common causes will be the quality of the barrel steel and heat treatment of the barrel.

It's a simple matter to stone the build-up off the cutting edge, simply use a knife edge stone or a diamond lap that will fit inside the flute. Lay it along the cutting surface of the flute and stone lightly to remove the metal that has welded to the cutting edge.

Be sure to keep your stone flat on the inside of the flute so you do not dull or change the angle of the flute. Stoning in this manner removes very little in terms of the diameter of the reamer because of the geometry of the cutting edge. Never stone on the periphery of the reamer as this changes the dimensions of the reamer rapidly.

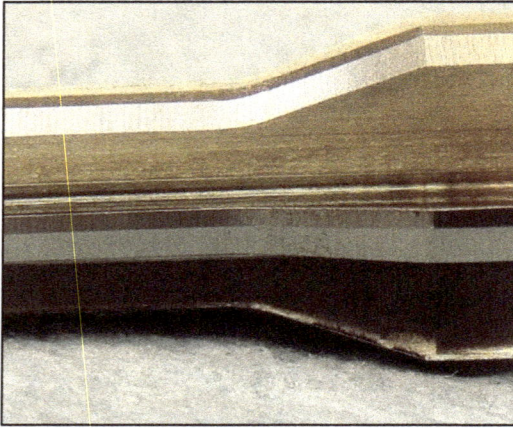

Above we see a reamer with metal build-up (chip welding) on the shoulder, bottom cutting edge in the picture. There is no damage to the cutting edge itself.

Determining Bore Diameter:

Since we just discussed pilot diameter on reamers there are probably a few of you saying, "But how do I know what size pilot I really need?"

It's important to understand at this point the difference between nominal bore diameter and actual bore diameter. We are only interested in the actual bore diameter as this is what the pilot will be working against the barrel to align the reamer.

Nominal bore diameter is the standard for caliber bore diameter that most folks assume is the diameter; i.e. .308 caliber barrels have a nominal bore diameter of .300" So a standard pilot is .299" to .2995". Now the monkey wrench in the works… Not all makers produce standard diameter barrels, so you have to measure to be sure.

Note: the bore is the diameter measured across the lands of the barrel or the smallest bore dimension inside the barrel.

Some makers mark the bore diameter on the breech of the barrel, if you have experience with the maker and know they are marking the real dimension then by all means you can use that information. More commonly, they mark either the nominal caliber or the nominal minimum and maximum dimensions of the bore, i.e. bore and groove diameters.

Hole gauges can be used but they are not terribly precise unless you are very experienced in using and measuring them. The simplest way to measure the diameter of the bore is to utilize pin gauges. Such gauges can be purchased in sets at relatively low cost. Simply use them as go and no-go, they come in .001" increments so the correct diameter will go, the next size up will not or will enter only with resistance. As with all such precision tools never force it.

It is also possible to "slug" the bore. This process is a low tech method that is very accurate.

To Slug a Barrel:

Items needed are two rods that will easily slip inside the bore of the barrel. One short and one long, more on this later. A small piece of soft lead near the diameter of the bore. Keep the rods within 1/16" of the bore diameter, this protect the bore from the rods marking or gouging the interior of the barrel.

Drill rod is excellent for this purpose as it is ground on the exterior and stiff so it is not likely to bend and cause any problems. Bevel both ends of the rod slightly to remove any burrs that might cut you or scratch the barrel.

Push an oily patch through the barrel to wet the surface of the bore. You are looking for lubrication for the lead slug, not so much oil that its dripping on your foot. Just a tight fitting oily patch passed through the bore will do. Any gun oil is acceptable for this purpose.

As for the lead as long as it is soft, not alloyed bullet material, it will form nicely. Soft lead balls, cast bullet cores, lead wire are all good options for this. Often times oversized lead balls are the easiest source of material, if you're a muzzle loader you probably already have them.

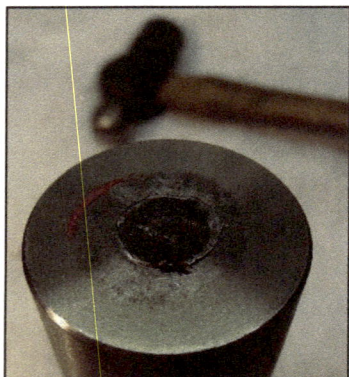

Simply place the ball on the opening to the bore. Tapping it into the bore with a ball peen hammer is perfectly acceptable. Here we are working on a barrel blank so there is no danger of wrecking a crown or the chamber etc. If you're working on a finished barrel use more finesse.

At left: The smudge that is visible around the slug is from the thin material that was swaged out as the slug was tapped into the bore. In this picture the excess material has been removed.

Once the lead is swagged very thin at the end of the barrel you can use one of the rods to push the slug into the bore further and peel off the thin material that is left at the end of the barrel as it would be in the way.

Push the slug a few inches into the bore. Place the longer rod in the bore until it touches the slug. You need that rod to be long enough so that it's still protruding from the end of the barrel. It will become the anvil, use the shorter rod to smash the piece of lead. The idea is that the lead is trapped between the anvil and a hammer (the two rods). The anvil needs to rest on a hard surface, a steel plate on a concrete floor works great.

Make sure the short rod is far enough in the bore so that you cannot angle it toward the inside wall of the barrel, we don't want to damage rifling… Use an 18 ounce or heavier hammer to strike the short rod and upset the lead slug between it and the anvil rod. A few good bumps will do it.

Now here is what makes this method useful to the gunsmith and the reloader. We remove the rods from the barrel, insert the long rod and push the slug through the bore. This will likely take some effort and may even require the use of mallet to move the slug. The slug is forced down the bore and will be conformed to the smallest point in the bore, both for the bore and the groove diameters. If there are noticeable loose spots or areas of high resistance to movement then you have a barrel that is not very uniform end to end that would benefit from lapping.

The resulting slug can be used to measure the diameters the bore and the groove. Remember it is a mirror image of the inside of your barrel.

At Right: Slug and rod, be careful not to bevel too much it could become a wedge and get stuck in the bore.

Bore Scopes for better or worse:

The advent of bore scopes has been invaluable to the gunsmith's ability to diagnose problems inside the bore of the barrel or in the chamber area. There is a clear down side to this tool however. The most popular brand of bore scope has about a sixteen power magnification. This allows us to see details that do not actually play into accuracy, so the untrained eye will see minuscule flaws in the barrel and assume they represent problems.

Most of the tiny marks are minor or cosmetic flaws in the bore and are a source of great controversy between the gunsmith and the client. I have seen barrels that were shooting well under minute of angle come back because somebody looked through a bore scope and saw a shiny spot, a tool mark or a burr from the manufacturing process.

To become educated on the use of a bore scope, look at lots of barrels. So that you can recognize what is acceptable and what is a real concern. Many end users think that the bore must appear perfect to produce accuracy. To this I would simply say, prove it at the range!

Why the side trip into bore scopes?

Solid pilot reamers will sometimes burnish or polish a small area ahead of the throat where they rub. If this burnishing does not dimensionally change the bore, and in most cases it does not, then it's a *non-issue*. In fact, within 100 shots it will be gone in most cases. And, 100 shots is about the normal amount for a break-in period on the barrel. If the marks caused by the pilot are deeper than that, then the pilot is too large for the bore, so it should not have been used with that particular barrel in the first place.

To summarize, if your pilot is properly matched to the bore, i.e. .001" smaller than the bore, then you have the best relationship between the bore and the tool. Such a close fit will help eliminate potential chatter. This close fit will also insure that the throat and chamber are properly aligned with the bore. If the bullet cannot enter the bore properly aligned it will never be accurate.

So if you ask which is better, a solid pilot or a removable pilot? I would have to say, that depends on the barrel you're using and your experience with the tools. Either can produce amazing accuracy, it's up to the gunsmith to set the job up correctly to get the most out of the barrel.

That Unsightly Bulge?

Or Does This Brass Make My Chamber Look Big?

When hunting season was just around the corner the local shooting range was a busy place. Each day dozens of hunters, young, old, male, or female all flood the range during the last few weekends before opening day. Their goal is to make sure that rifle is sighted in correctly so they can concentrate solely on game animals, wind direction, terrain, and all the variables that go into a successful hunt. Nobody wants to be wondering if their rifle is hitting where they point it.

On trips to the range at that time of year it's not unusual to find fired brass lying around. Over the years I have noticed that much of this brass can tell a story about the gun it came out of. Sort of a "CSI, Sighting in Days" can take place. There is a huge variation in the brass that you find laying around at the range. It can tell you about the manufacturer specifications, cleanliness, quality, and overall condition of the firearm that fired the brass to name just a few things.

Just like in the TV show "CSI", we need to tell you what we are talking about in plain terms and attach that information to the correct nomenclature.

As a gunsmith I occasionally field questions about fire formed brass. Experience indicates that most shooters and reloaders have some misconceptions about reading brass in order to understand what is happening when the cartridge is fired. Often this is a result of confusion over the nomenclature of cartridge cases and their various features. Study the photos and identifications on the following page to understand proper nomenclature.

Often reloaders confuse head expansion with web expansion. Notice in the picture of the cut away brass at right that the solid head of the case does not normally expand. It's easy to see that the solid head is much tougher than the web or the body of the case by virtue of its thickness.

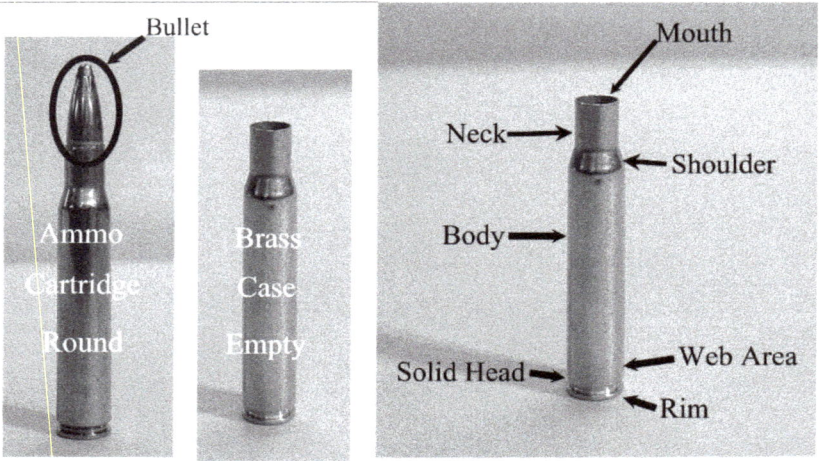

The reason that the brass tapers up to the maximum internal diameter area, indicated by the red arrow at right, is that the brass is thick near the solid head and tapers out to body thickness as you move towards the muzzle. This is both a by-product of the manufacturing process and serves the purpose of adding some strength to this portion of the case.

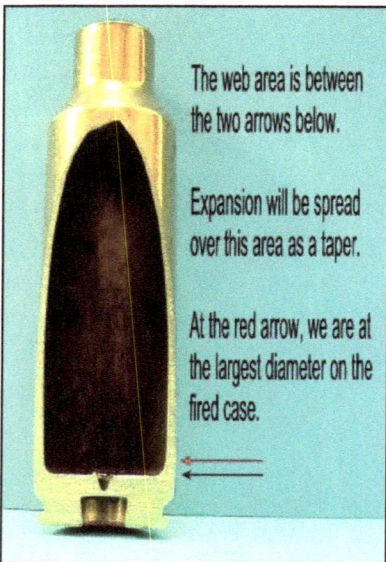

The web area is between the two arrows below.

Expansion will be spread over this area as a taper.

At the red arrow, we are at the largest diameter on the fired case.

Case head expansion as a method of checking the pressure of your loads was about the only method available to the average reloader in the past. This method involves measuring at the solid head. If the reloader did not understand the correct nomenclature he might think every load that expanded the web or body of the case was dangerous. It is not at all unusual to have clients point to the expanded web area and call it head expansion. The area below the black line in the photo is what is called the solid head.

The Sporting Arms and Ammunition Manufacturers' Institute (SAAMI) is an association of the nation's leading manufacturers of firearms, ammunition, and components. SAAMI was founded in 1926 at the request of the United States, Federal government and tasked with:

- ✓ Creating and publishing industry standards for safety, interchangeability, reliability and quality

- ✓ Coordinating technical data

- ✓ Promoting safe and responsible firearms use

In order for SAAMI to meet its stated goals it is necessary for them to allow a range of measurements or specification, known in the manufacturing business as tolerances. These tolerances apply both to the ammunition and the firearms that are designed to use them. Both length and diameter have tolerances, so it is possible to have ammunition that is fairly small in relation to the chamber; and a chamber that is on the large end of tolerances, thus requiring the brass to make up a lot of distance. The standards set by SAAMI take these variations into consideration to assure safe operation of firearms and ammo made by all manufacturers no matter which brands you might combine. But that does not mean it will always look good when brass is fire formed.

Brass from five (5) guns of various calibers were selected at random for this explanation. Four sets are fired unsized cases and the fifth set is resized fired cases. Three pieces of brass from each gun were gathered so that we could get an average for that gun. Brass is manufactured to the aforementioned tolerances; consequently it will have to expand to fill the chamber. Brass is malleable and is intended to stretch and adapt the specific chamber it is fired in.

Let's look at the 30-06 as an example as it is fairly representative of all bottleneck cases. According to SAAMI specifications the diameter of the cartridge can be .008" smaller than the standard dimension at any point along the body as compared to the chamber. Length measurements are allowed to vary almost twice that much, at .015". On diameter alone the base of the brass could measure as small as .4618" at the same time the chamber can be .002" larger than standard specification, so that would be .4728" a gap of .011" in diameter. That's a lot of stretching for the brass to do, but it is totally capable of the job, and it would all be within allowed SAAMI tolerance.

Logically, manufacturers will order their dies for the making of brass cases at the minimum specifications. That way as the dies wear they will not exceed the maximum allowable dimensions. Also brass made toward the minimum specifications will then work well in all chambers. Reloading is not a main concern for the brass and ammunition maker; rather reliability and safety rank the highest in consideration.

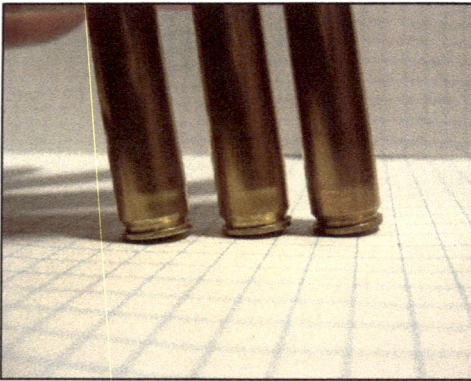

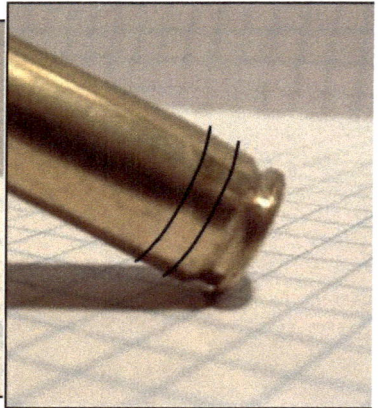

On the left, you can see the bulged area on the body, the line you see is actually ahead of the web area slightly, where the brass is thin enough for it to balloon out. At right is an 06 case, the line closest to the head marks the end of the solid head, the second line, toward the muzzle, is the end of the web area. So the largest diameter on this case is at or above the upper line (closer to the muzzle), actually a point on the body is being measured.

At left, you can see that our sample of 300 Winchester Short Magnum (WSM) shows the same evidence of expansion.

Chamber tools ordered by the gun manufacturers will normally come in with the maximum allowable dimensions. That way as they wear or are sharpened they will last much longer, both saving money and insuring function of the chamber with all ammo.

Brass Measurements Averages			
Manufacturer	Caliber	Solid Head Diameter	Web Area Diameter
Winchester	30-06	0.4640"	0.4705"
Federal	300 WSM	0.5524"	0.560"
Speer Nickel	300 Weatherby	0.5096"	0.5129"
Remington	300 RUM	0.5480"	0.5521"
Remington	338-06 *(resized)*	0.4643"	0.4677"

Sometimes a reloader will notice this expansion and often it is lop-sided, in other words, more expansion on one side of the case than on the other. It could be that the chamber is out of round, but it is far more likely that the brass has a thin side and stretches to fill the chamber when fired; the brass swelled up to fill the difference between the chamber and the ammo where there was more room. So, don't panic.

Measure your brass along the body; it should be concentrically round where it has expanded to meet the chamber walls. If it is, then the lop-sided shape of the brass at the base is because of the thin

spot stretching first or the extractor pushing the cartridge to one side, not an oblong chamber. I discussed this with Gordy and he said he had watched for this phenomenon when testing guns and found that the expansion we are discussing is random, never happening in the exact same part of the chamber which totally supports the concept that it is the thin or weak point in the brass that allows this expansion.

It is not unusual when you measure the body to find minor eccentricities of a couple 1/10000 of an inch, i.e. .0001" to .0002" these anomalies are equally as likely to be intrinsic to the brass itself as it is to the chamber. As brass contracts after firing it will move more in thin areas than in thick, thus creating minor variances.

Accuracy buffs will not like the facts portrayed here, but the experienced ones have learned these details long ago. There are many ways to deal with this as a reloader; that is not the point of this chapter though. Instead, we are trying to help gunsmiths and reloaders understand some of the variables found in chambers, brass, and ammunition. With this knowledge you should be better suited to reload accurate ammo.

Headspace Gauges

Headspace gauges are designed to establish the correct and precise length of the chamber, no matter the type of cartridge.

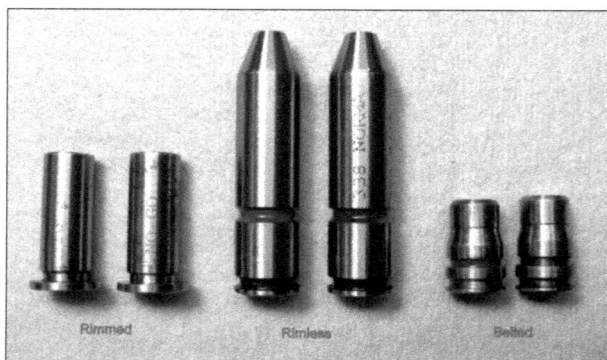

Standard Styles of Headspace Gauges

Correct headspace is define by a gauge in contact with the breech face of the bolt in the fully locked or closed position; At the same time the datum point on the gauge must be touching the datum point in the chamber. This information is set by SAAMI for U.S. cartridges and by C.I.P. for European calibers.

In the case of wildcats a reamer maker will assist the designer with headspace gauges if they do not know how to establish gauging for their chamber.

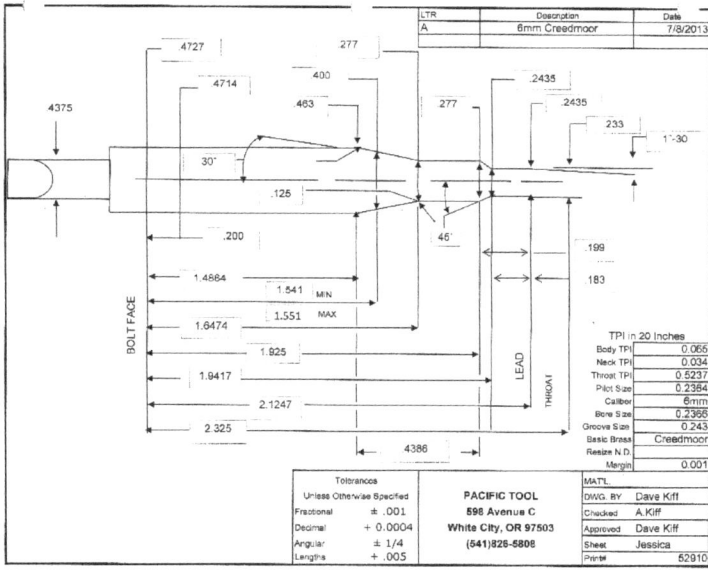

Note the point on the shoulder that is .400" in diameter, that is the datum line for this cartridge. Then the Min & Max numbers are the established headspace length for this cartridge. A Go-Gauge would be made to minimum length, a Field Gauge to maximum and an No-Go about half way between, normally about .004" longer than the Go-Gauge.

For an in depth and complete discussion of headspace see our title, "Understanding Headspace" #2 in the "Gunsmith Student Handbook Series".

Part II

Extreme Accuracy Chambering
by Gordy Gritters

In the world of extreme-accuracy gunsmithing, there are several ways that gunsmiths chamber rifle barrels for accuracy. If you are detail-oriented, take the time and care to use good well-tuned actions, properly bedded stocks, top-quality barrels and make sure you're dialing them in properly, anyone can turn out extremely accurate rifles, right from their very first one. I've seen this too many times to believe otherwise after having guys with little or no experience take my classes, then go home, practice what they've learned, and immediately start building great shooting rifles.

I will explain my preferred chambering method that takes a slightly different approach than more historically traditional methods due to the issues I found with those methods. I am going to explain the issues I found with the traditional methods, and the methodology I used to test for and overcome these issues. I will explain how I cut different dimension necks and throats in the chamber to match what the customer needs for specific applications. I will go over how I set my lathe up to be able to dial-in bores very accurately, as well as some of the tooling and indicators I use for this. Finally at the end, I have included a step-by-step chambering section, explaining each step of the process in great detail from start to finish.

I started my gunsmithing business back in 1987, and building/accurizing rifles soon became what I specialized in. I chamber barrels and build rifles for all types of usage, including 600 and 1000 yard long-range benchrest rifles, short-range benchrest rifles, F-class rifles, many other types of match rifles, tactical rifles, sniper rifles, long-range varmint rifles, and all types of hunting rifles.

The barrel contours, twist rates, and cartridges being chambered will vary depending on the bullets used, and how the customer will be using his rifle. The chamber dimensions, including the neck and throat, will vary depending on what will be optimum for each particular rifle being built. But I use basically the same method for all chambering, regardless of how it will be used. I teach this method in much greater detail in the precision rifle-building and chambering classes I conduct periodically in my shop.

Sometimes the method a gunsmith uses to chamber barrels is dictated by the type of equipment he is using. One example of this is he will not be able to chamber barrels by the "through-the-headstock" method if his lathe's headstock has a small spindle bore, in which case he will likely chamber between centers. Other times a gunsmith may prefer another one of the accepted methods that has worked well in the past, and if it is a method that a lot of other top gunsmiths use, this can be a good way to do things. One of the most well-known methods here is dialing both ends of the bore to run true, at the throat and at the crown. This "dial-in both ends" method works very well and is still used today by a lot of the world's top gunsmiths, and most of their barrels shoot very well.

In the past I've tried all different methods to chamber barrels. I tried chambering barrels between centers, but was unable to get the bore dialed-in accurately enough to suit me using that method. No matter how I re-cut the centers or supported the barrel, I could never get rid of measureable run-out, plus I was not able to articulate the curvature of the bore to dial it the way I wanted unless I used a hand-made "spider" that I mounted in the steady-rest. Then it worked OK, but took a lot of extra dialing-in time.

I used the "dial-in both ends" method for many years with great success. This is one of the best traditional methods to use, but I found that this method also has issues that I do not like. Years ago, when I bought my first Hawkeye borescope, I noticed right away that some throats did not appear to be as perfectly aligned to the bore as I thought they should be, even though I had both ends of the bore, at the throat and at the crown, dialed to within .0001". I soon found that the imperfect-looking throats were always in barrels that had quite a bit of curvature in the bore. This is because the chamber will be machined in line with the lathe bed, but due to bore curvature, the bore directly ahead of the chamber is not in line with the lathe bed – therefore the chamber will not be in line with the bore using this method!

In my experience, no barrel has a perfectly straight bore. I have dialed-in and measured thousands of barrels over the years - a few have come close, but I have never found one that was perfectly straight.

So in the "dial both ends" method where you indicate both ends of a bore to be running true only at the throat and at the crown, the bore WILL be curved in between those two points, and therefore the bore WILL be coming to the chamber and to the crown at a slight angle. The more curvature in the bore, the worse the angle to the chamber and crown becomes - this really bothers me!

These drawings are exaggerated to show what is going on. *The full-length red centerline in both drawings is the alignment of the lathe – and therefore this will also be the alignment of the chamber and the action threads*

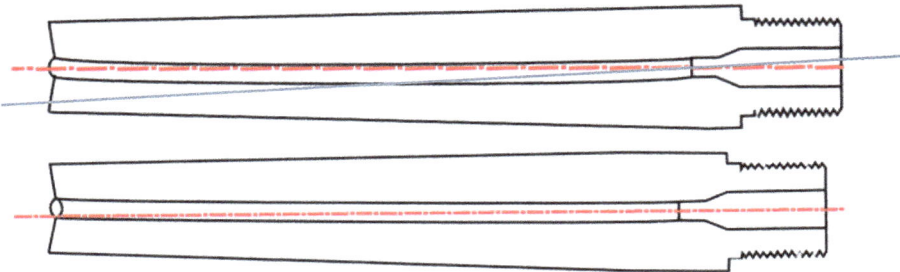

Upper barrel shows "Dial both ends" method. The angled blue line shows the centerline of the bore where it meets the chamber when using the "dial both ends" method - note that the bore is misaligned to the chamber when dialing-in the curved bore at both ends with this method

Lower barrel shows "Dial chamber straight to bore" method – note how the chamber is perfectly aligned to the beginning of the bore. The bore curvature at the muzzle end is then aligned to be "up" or "down", never to the side. Much better results!

After much testing, and chambering both ways myself over the years, I have come to the definite opinion that I prefer dialing in barrels to get the beginning section of bore just ahead of the throat to align perfectly straight to the chamber. The *"Dial chamber straight to bore"* method eliminates <u>all</u> of the crooked throat issues I used to see, and in my opinion it gives a slight accuracy edge over any other method I have tried.

Even though my preferred method of dialing-in bores may be a little more difficult to learn and may take a few minutes longer until you get used to it, to me it is worth the extra effort since it aligns the chamber to the bore better than other methods. I strive to do everything I possibly can to give an accuracy edge for my customers when I build their rifles, even if it takes a little longer.

The chamber–to-bore misalignment I was seeing when using these other methods really bothered me, so I did a lot of testing and evaluation trying to figure out what was going on. Every time I finish a chamber I always double-check my work with a borescope and by measuring for run-out with my .0001" long-reach dial test indicator. I would always get zero or near-zero run-out through the body of the chamber, the neck and the freebore part of the throat – this always measured perfect.

But one day I moved the indicator forward into the bore 1/2" ahead of the throat, and found that the indicator showed some run-out. When I moved farther forward and measured 1" ahead of the throat, the run-out was measurably more, and the further forward I went the worse the run-out became. What in the world was going on?

This meant the bore directly ahead of the chamber was obviously running at a slight angle to the chamber itself, which was a big problem for me! I quickly figured out it was because of the curvature of the bore. I thought this had to be adversely affecting the accuracy a little, and now after changing my methods and seeing the results I am absolutely convinced of it. I have found after starting to use my new "Dial chamber straight to bore" method of dialing in chambers, it works extremely well and better yet, the chambers, the throats, and the bore just ahead of the throat all now measure and align perfectly straight and true <u>every time without fail</u>!

Action Prep: Before we get into the details of extreme-accuracy chambering, we have to make sure the action is not going to detract from the expected level of accuracy. I'm only going to touch on a few things about the action here, but these things definitely make a difference on the rifles accuracy.

First and foremost is having good bolt lug contact on all the lugs, whether it's 2, 3, 4, 6, or 9 lugs – they all must have some contact so the bolt pushes back evenly against all the action lug seats when the gun is fired to prevent action/barrel flexing. You don't need 100% lug contact, 50-75% contact or more on each lug is fine.

Most factory actions and even most custom actions have contact on only one lug when I check the lug contact with red Magic Marker on the back of the bolt lugs. I expect this in most factory actions, but why do more than 90% of custom actions come with only one lug touching, and zero contact on one or more of the other lugs? One reason is that the bolts and the receivers are machined straight and true in the manufacturer's CNC machines, but the bolt and the receiver are not sitting straight to each other when the rifle is cocked and fired.

In a custom action, if the stripped bolt is slid into the raceway of the bare receiver and you check the lug contact now, both lugs (I'll assume a 2-lug action here, but 3-lug or more actions are the same) will usually have some contact with the lug seats in the receiver, so most people think it's OK as-is (if they even bother to check it). But the problem is this is not how the parts are contacting each other when the rifle is cocked and fired.

First off, the weight of the barrel hanging from the front of the action flexes the action. So whenever possible, I check and correct the bolt lug contact with the gun upright and held by the stock, supported just like it will be when it is fired, since the lug contact can change with the weight of the barrel flexing the action.

When the action is cocked, the bolt lugs are pushed back against the lug seats by the firing pin spring, and the rear of the bolt is forced up against the top of the bolt bore raceway of the receiver by the trigger. The bottom bolt lug becomes the pivot point when the rear of the bolt being forced up pulls the top lug off its seat, <u>so the bolt is not aligned straight in the receiver when it's cocked</u>.

The looser the bolt is in the bolt bore raceway of the receiver, the farther the rear of the bolt comes up, and the farther the top lug comes off its seat. This is one reason why looser, sloppier actions don't shoot as accurately as tighter ones. When the rifle is fired, the bolt is pushed back hard by the rapidly expanding cartridge, forcing the bottom lug to bear hard against its seat a split second before the top one does. The bottom lug pushing hard against its seat flexes the action there first, followed by the top lug slapping hard and fast against its lug seat, creating an unwanted vibration. Since the barrel is attached to the action directly ahead of this, the action flexing induces a whip/vibration in the barrel right while the bullet is going through the bore, which definitely hurts accuracy.

So to obtain the most accuracy and shot to shot uniformity that I can, I first reduce the amount of bolt play in the action by one of

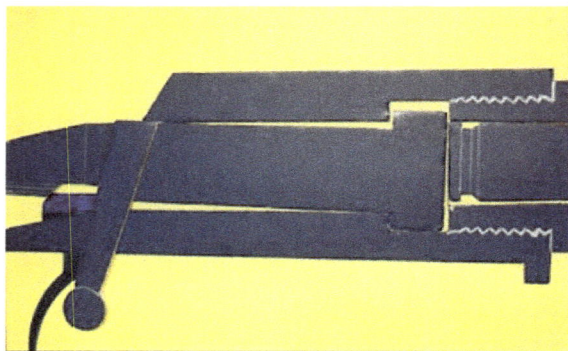

This image shows what happens in a typical factory action or loose custom action – when rifle is cocked, rear of bolt is forced up, pulling upper bolt lug off its seat, and bolt face is not square to the cartridge, all of which hurts accuracy! Even after bolt lugs are lapped, when the bolt is sloppy in the action, the lug contact is not very uniform from one shot to the next

these three methods: (1) replacing the bolt with one that is larger diameter, (2) by sleeving the original bolt with steel sleeves to enlarge its body diameter, or (3) by reducing the inside diameter of the bolt bore raceway with a thin layer of epoxy (what I call "epoxy-sleeving" the action). I have produced a DVD showing this method of "epoxy-sleeving" to reduce bolt play in an action, and how to properly lap bolt lugs so the lugs all have contact in the cocked position.

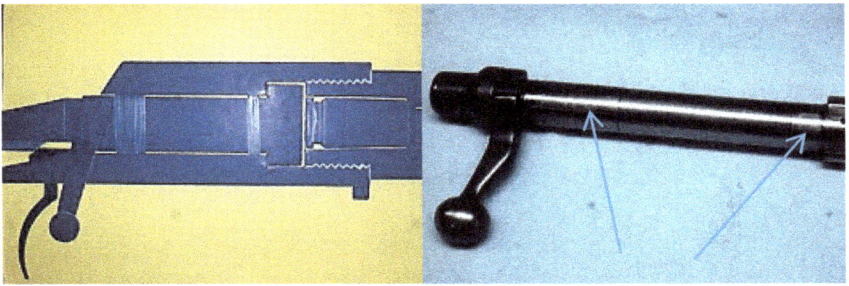

This image depicts the advantage of a close tolerance custom action or minimizing bolt play in a factory action. Bolt lugs maintain uniform contact with the lug seats much better shot after shot, which helps accuracy!

Sleeved factory bolt – steel sleeves on bolt body increase diameter to minimize bolt play in action

I feel this step is absolutely critical! I <u>install the trigger and lap the bolt lugs with the bolt in the cocked position</u>, which is the exact position it is in when the rifle is fired. Lapping lugs so they have good contact with the lug seats in the cocked position not only makes sure <u>all</u> the bolt lugs are against their seats and eliminates as much bolt movement as possible when the gun is fired, but most important, the end result is that this reduces the amount of action/barrel flex and vibration while the bullet is going through the bore, which is where the real accuracy gains come from.

Other common accurizing procedures, like truing the receiver face, lug seats, receiver threads, bolt face, etc, also help accuracy to some degree. It is important to make sure the firing pin, and all bolt parts operate smoothly, and that nothing is loose, bent, dragging against other parts, or in a bind. Remove the firing pin spring and reassemble the bolt without the spring, then make sure the firing pin and cocking piece slides forward and back freely without anything binding or dragging – correct anything that is.

Another thing that's not so well known is to make sure that there is enough firing pin travel and spring tension to get reliable ignition, which can hurt accuracy if either is too minimal. One person who did extensive testing in a rail gun that proved the correlation of good ignition to top accuracy was Greg Whalley of Kelbly Actions. I'm not going to take time here to go into all the ways this can be checked and corrected, but I'll explain one simple test you can do to check ignition energy.

Place an unloaded, primed case in the chamber, then lower the bolt very gently while holding the trigger back so the firing pin goes down against the primer without firing it. Measure the cocking piece location in the shroud and write this figure down. Then cock the action and pull the trigger so it fires the primer. Now without opening the bolt, measure where the cocking piece is located now – how far has it penetrated into the primer while firing? In most cases you want to have about .020" or more of primer penetration to give good ignition. If you only have let's say .015" or so, it may not misfire, but your accuracy will probably be better by installing a heavier firing pin spring, by increasing the firing pin travel, or in some cases by increasing the weight of the firing pin itself – all of which will give more striking energy against the primer.

Lathe Setup: Now, let's talk about setting up a lathe for "through the headstock" chambering. Several years ago I helped Grizzly design their "gunsmith lathes", which are designed to be capable of high accuracy chambering work. Now you can purchase a gunsmith lathe from companies such as Grizzly, Shop Fox, or Precision Matthews that are already set up for through-the-headstock chambering work, or you can modify a standard lathe for this purpose. You really want to have a good smooth-running lathe that has high quality bearings and gears, with the bearings adjusted properly to take the end-play out of the headstock.

A high-quality big, heavy engine lathe mounted on a one-piece cast-iron base will be very stiff and ideal for doing this type of work, but a decent quality lighter-duty lathe will work just fine as long as you use good sharp tooling and take lighter cuts. I've chambered a number of barrels on light-duty lathes like the smaller Grizzly and Precision Matthews gunsmith lathes when I've traveled to other shops to conduct private gunsmithing classes. These little lathes have been able to turn out surprisingly good work, so I'm never afraid to recommend them to folks on a budget.

One of the primary things needed in a gunsmith lathe will be a large enough spindle bore through the headstock to allow side-clearance for the barrel to be dialed in. I recommend the spindle bore be <u>at least .060"-.080" larger</u> than the largest barrel you will be working on, and .100" larger would be better. For example – a lathe with a 1 9/16" spindle bore can easily dial-in 1.450" diameter 1000-yard barrels and even up to most 1.500" barrels.

Another thing you really want is a headstock narrow enough so shorter barrels can be supported at both ends of the headstock and still have enough barrel sticking out of the chuck to work on. If your lathe doesn't have a narrow enough headstock or a large enough spindle bore, don't worry since there is still a way to dial-in barrels accurately. I recommend using a jig something like GreTan's action truing fixture or Bob Pastor's Viper chambering fixture, which was designed for dialing-in and chambering short barrels. I've used my GreTan action jig for years to dial-in and chamber short barrels (see photo below) and for very accurately dialing-in and chambering custom dies.

Left: GreTan action truing jig, which also works quite well for chambering short barrels and custom dies

Right: Viper action truing and chambering jig

These jigs both work well for chambering short barrels if you use sharp tooling and take light cuts

Chambering a short barrel in a GreTan action truing jig

There is a new and very innovative system recently on the market called the TrueBore Alignment system, which I have just recently started to use. I find it especially useful for truing actions and chambering short barrels.

SSG's True Bore Alignment System is an innovative way to dial in barrels and actions. The part can be completely dialed-in using just the adjustments and articulation built into this unit

If your lathe is not already set up for the "through the headstock" method of supporting and articulating the bore to dial it in accurately, you will have to modify it to do so. In this method, you set the barrel up through the headstock of the lathe, supporting the chamber end of the barrel in a 4-jaw chuck or "spider-chuck", and supporting the outboard end of the barrel with 4 opposing screws or a "spider" on the outboard end of the headstock spindle. I modified the outboard end of my headstock spindle into a "spider" by drilling/tapping the spindle for 4 opposing screws, in effect making it into a secondary 4-jaw chuck to support/adjust the outboard end of the barrel.

Outboard end of headstock spindle can be tapped for four opposing screws, making it into a "spider" for dialing-in barrels using the "through the headstock" chambering method. You may have to fabricate a "spider" to install on your lathe

This lets me infinitely adjust the barrel at both ends in any direction, and gives me complete control of articulating the bore ahead of the throat to align it the way I want. To do this I simply adjust the muzzle end of the barrel slightly off-center at the outboard end of the lathe, just enough to get the first 1 ½ or 2 inches of bore ahead of the chamber to align straight and true to the axis of the lathe.

You must put small shims between your chuck jaws and the barrel to allow your barrel to "pivot" in the chuck jaws when off-setting the outboard end of the barrel. I use L-shaped aluminum shims that extend only about 3/16" to 1/4" under the front edge of the chuck jaws to support the barrel. Any longer than that and the flat of your chuck jaws will not let your barrel pivot in the chuck to be dialed in properly. I prefer to use aluminum for the shims, since you don't have to tighten the chuck jaws so tight to keep the barrel from slipping, and they don't mar a finished part easily, which I like.

Use small aluminum shims under the front edges of the chuck jaws to allow the barrel to be articulated while dialing the bore straight and true

A foot brake is not mandatory, but is sure a nice feature to have, especially handy when cutting metric threads, and on the rare occasion that you have an unexpected problem where you need to stop the lathe quickly. It also saves time to be able to stop the lathe quickly after each threading or chambering pass, instead of shutting it down and having to wait for the lathe to wind down to a stop each time!

On my lathe, I also modified the tailstock hold-down lever to accept a torque wrench. This modification is thanks to Greg Tannel from GreTan Rifles/GTR Tooling. This allows me to tighten the tailstock lever to the exact torque it takes to get the centerline of the tailstock to vertically align exactly with the centerline of the headstock, which is a nice feature if your tailstock is not too high to do this.

Torque wrench added to the tailstock hold-down lever. This is used to tighten the tailstock to the exact amount needed to align the tailstock vertically to the headstock

First, level the bed of your lathe straight and true with a high precision machine level, then you can measure and find out exactly how much torque on the tailstock hold-down clamp it takes to align the tailstock centerline to the headstock centerline. Tailstocks can be easily adjusted horizontally to bring them into alignment, but some lathes are quite a ways off vertically and can take a lot of work and expense to get the tailstock to align vertically to the headstock – you better know what you are doing before you try to correct this. If your lathe tailstock is made too high (very common) and when tightened down fully it still is off more than .001" - .002"

or so, don't sweat it, just know that you'll have to use a floating reamer holder instead of a fixed reamer holder like the GreTan holder I like to use.

Thankfully both my lathes came into alignment without any expensive modifications, so all I had to do was just figure out the proper torque specs for each one. The first lathe I set up for chambering this way took 12 ft/lbs of torque to align perfectly and my current chambering lathe takes 20 ft/lbs.

Dialing-in methods: When the action work is done, it's time to start chambering the barrel. I use one of two methods to true the section of bore directly ahead of the chamber – the "direct-reading method" and the "range-rod method".   Either way, I start by setting the barrel up through the headstock, dial it somewhat close to true (within .001"-.002" or so) then pre-drill the chamber before finishing the dialing-in process. Pre-drilling the chamber at this time allows the indicator to reach far enough into the bore of most chambers to dial them in using the "direct reading method". After the chamber hole is pre-drilled, I'll then finish dialing-in the bore before chambering the barrel.

Direct-reading method: The primary method I use for most chambers is to simply reach in with my Mitotoyu .0001" dial test indicator with a 1.500" long point to direct read in the grooves near the throat and then forward 1.500", which is as far as the point can reach. The forward body of this indicator is .375" diameter, which will be able to reach into the chamber hole of most chambers 1.500", with the point extending forward another 1.500" from there – works great for dialing-in barrels! I use a 2.675" long indicator point on chambers when the 1.500" point won't reach far enough, but this reduces the indicator sensitivity to around .0004", making it a little harder to get dialed-in as close as I want. Then I go back and forth in this area dialing and adjusting the barrel until this section of the bore runs perfectly straight and true.

Whenever possible, I do feel it is better to indicate in the grooves of the bore rather than on top of the lands. The grooves make up the largest percentage of the bore, and are what supports and guides the bullet. The lands are almost always the same height, but I have seen barrels that had slightly different height lands. This isn't common, but it can happen.

The lands compress into the bullet, but the grooves are what actually support and guide the rotational mass of the bullet, so this outer surface of the bullet is what I want to be running true. The reamer bushing rides on the tops of the lands, but if you dial the bore true, and pre-drill/true the chamber hole first, the chamber reamer will follow the trued chamber hole, and the chamber and throat will align dead-true to the grooves of the bore ahead of it, even if the tops of the lands aren't perfect (reamer flex comes into play here).

Range rod method: For the second method, I use what I call a "range rod" to start the process. I use these rods especially for small diameter chambers that the .375" diameter body of my indicator is too large to go into (like 222, 223, etc), or for extra-long chambers (like 300 RUM, 338 Lapua, etc) where the chamber is too long to use this indicator with the 1.500" point. I sometimes dial it in directly using a 2.675" point on my indicator, but since this reduces the indicator sensitivity so much, I generally prefer the range rod to do that.

I hold one end of the rod in the tailstock chuck so it does not turn with the barrel, and put the other end of the rod with a close-fitting reamer bushing (ideally within .0002" or so) into the bore just ahead of the chamber (make sure it's not tight in the bore and is lubricated with oil so it slides easily). I place my .0001" dial indicator against the rod near where it enters the barrel, and measure vertical or side-to-side movement/flexing of the rod as I rotate the barrel.

If the bore has run-out, when you rotate the barrel the off-center bore will force the rod to move with it, which is easy to measure. When the bore is dialed-in and running true, the rod quits moving as the barrel is rotated. Then I move the rod/bushing forward and back 2" from the throat area of the bore, dialing and adjusting the barrel until this first section of the bore runs perfectly straight and true. I'll go into more detail on how to do this after a bit.

I tried the different types of range rods that were out there, but found issues with these. The ones that had tapers that went into the throat or rear of bore were not repeatable for me – they would measure differently every time I removed and re-inserted them, plus the taper would pull the rod off-center if it went into a crooked throat or bore entrance, which was not good.

The rods with two bushings worked OK most of the time, but only if you have two of every size bushing, and both bushings must fit the bore rather closely. Both of these types of rods have to be perfectly straight to even come close to working correctly – drop or bump one and it's most likely ruined.

After a lot of experimenting and testing, I developed a range rod that would give me repeatable accuracy, and was long enough to work even in barrels chambered in longer cartridges. Since it is not turning with the barrel, it even works fine if the rod is not straight, or is held in an unaligned tailstock. This is the only rod that I found to be repeatable enough to get acceptable accuracy using just the rod to dial-in a bore for chambering.

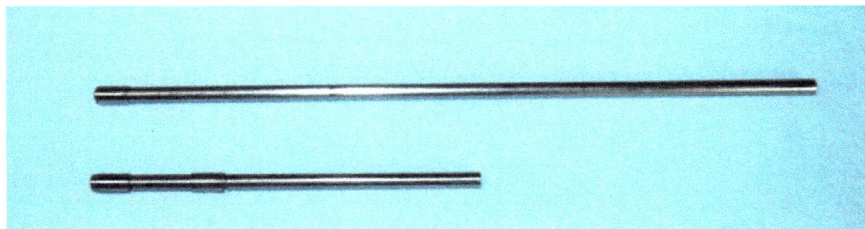

Longer range rod on top is the "Grizzly rod" with one bushing that I designed for dialing-in barrels using the "Dial chamber straight to bore" method. During extensive testing, it proved to be consistently much more accurate and repeatable than any other rod on the market

Shorter rod on bottom is a range rod with two bushings that I had PTG make for me quite a few years ago - it uses 2 dial indicators on the rod similar to dialing in an action, and worked OK as long as both bushings fit the bore snugly, and not well if the bushings did not fit the bore closely

The range rod I developed for this is a 12" - 13" long rod with a floating reamer bushing on one end, and the other end of the rod is held in the tailstock chuck so it does not turn. Reamer-maker Pacific Tool and Gauge calls it a "Grizzly rod" because it's the rod

I used when we made the Grizzly chambering DVD. For simplicity I call all these types of rods "range rods" but the reamer manufacturers call different types of rods by different names (range rods, indicator rods, Grizzly rods, etc) to keep them straight for ordering purposes. The Grizzly rod and reamer bushings in an assortment of sizes in .0002" increments can be purchased through Pacific Tool and Gauge or Dave Manson Precision Reamers.

I like to use bushings about .0002" smaller than bore for an easy slip-fit. The bore <u>absolutely must</u> be dialed-in extremely straight just ahead of the chamber to run bushings that close, or they can damage the tops of the lands when sliding in and out of the bore.

This photo shows the setup using the "Grizzly rod"

A properly fitted bushing on the end of the Grizzly rod is in the bore, the end of the rod is held by the tailstock chuck so it doesn't turn with the barrel, and a .0001" indicator is on top of the rod as close to the barrel as possible. When barrel is rotated with the chuck, if bore has run-out the rod will move with the bore, and the indicator reads this rod movement. When the bore is dialed-in, the rod does not move no matter where the bushing is placed from the throat area up to 2" ahead of the throat.

But no matter the type of rod used, I look at the range rod as a "roughing-in tool" in most cases. The Grizzly rod gets the barrel dialed-in extremely close – close enough in most cases by itself, but because of clearance between the bushing and rod, and the bushing and bore, there can still sometimes be .0002" or .0003" run-out remaining. After dialing the bore with a range rod, I always reach in with my long-reach indicator and direct-read in the grooves to fine-tune any remaining run-out to zero at the throat, since this is so easy to do at this point.

One note here - the Mitotoyu .0001" dial test indicator comes with a .700" point, which is calibrated to give the true .0001" reading. When I switch this to the 1.500" point that I use for the majority of my dialing-in, it effectively almost cuts the resolution in half. So each mark on the indicator now equals about .0002", and going halfway between the marks equals 0001". In effect, this is no problem at all since I am measuring for near zero run-out. So when it reads half a mark or less on the indicator, it is around .0001" or less, which is what I can almost always get barrels dialed in to.

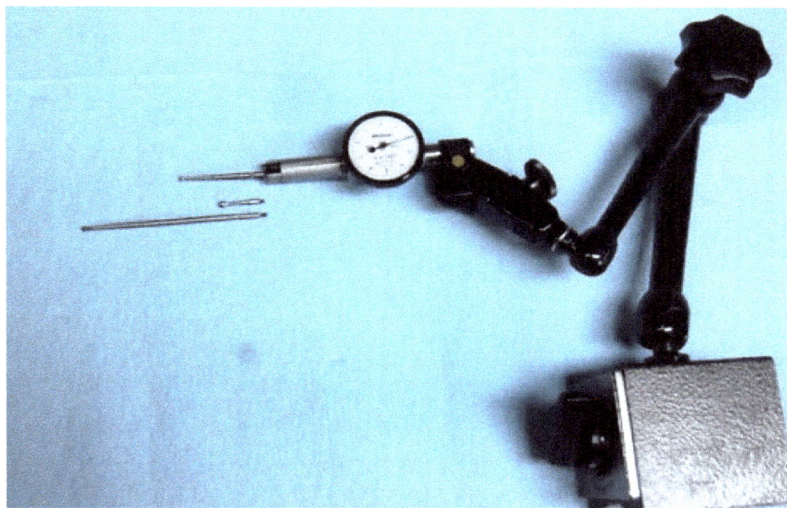

My preferred indicator setup: Mitotoyu .0001" indicator has a .375" diameter body which is small enough to enter most chambers for easy dialing-in. It comes with a .700" long point, and longer points such as these 1.500", and 2.675" points are available. Best tip diameter I have found for dialing-in bores is around .080". I like the Noga magnetic indicator holder with the fine-tune adjustment knob to use with this indicator

After pre-drilling the chamber, I dial the first 1.5"–2" of the bore ahead of the chamber straight and true. I then use a small boring bar to machine the pre-drilled chamber hole true, so it aligns dead-center to the bore directly ahead of it.

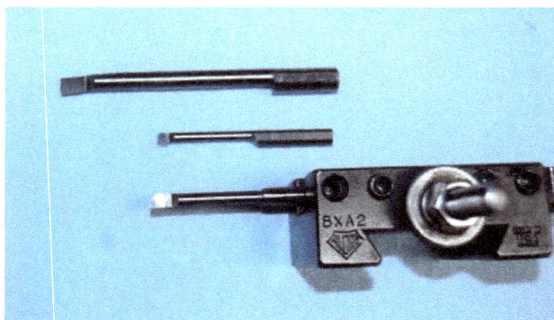

Small solid carbide boring bars for truing pre-drilled chamber holes, and for boring lands away in neck area of 5R barrels prior to chambering

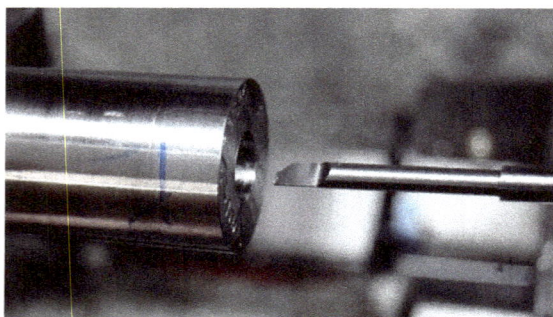

Getting ready to use a small carbide boring bar to bore the pre-drilled chamber hole true – do this after dialing the bore just ahead of the chamber straight and true

Now, when I chamber the barrel, the chamber reamer follows the bored/trued hole and aligns dead center to the bore ahead of it, and I get perfectly aligned chambers and throats every time.

When the chamber is finished, I can measure zero or near-zero run-out all the way through the chamber and throat, and it will continue to measure zero or near-zero run-out into the bore well ahead of the throat. This allows the bullet to align with and enter the bore perfectly straight, which will not reliably happen with any other method I've tried and tested. I have never found a better way to do this!

The same thing holds true when I have the barrel reversed in the lathe to cut a crown. When the last 1.5" - 2" of bore is aligned to run straight and true to the axis of the lathe when crowning a barrel, it makes for just a little straighter, truer crown, which helps accuracy.

A couple other quick notes here: The more curvature there is in a bore, the farther off-center the outboard end will run in the lathe, although it normally isn't by much. The slight amount of muzzle offset in the finished rifle you get by setting a barrel up like this is so minimal that you can never see the difference visually when the rifle is assembled.

Although I occasionally find a barrel that will run out almost .030" off-center at the outboard end (.060" total indicator reading), most custom barrels I've measured are somewhere in the .002"-.020" (.004" - .040" TIR) range.

I have seen a few custom barrels (and a lot of factory barrels) much worse than that, but it's very rare with custom barrels. I've measured and kept track of this curvature issue over quite a few years with my own barrels and a lot of my customer's barrels, but any normal amount of curvature doesn't seem to affect accuracy at all, as long as the chamber is aligned perfectly straight to the beginning part of the bore. I experimented years ago with trying to straighten custom barrels that had a lot of bore curvature, but this always killed the accuracy in "before and after" testing, so now if I feel there is a real problem with a barrel I will just return it to the barrel maker.

One thing I always do when fitting a barrel is to index (clock) barrels so the bore curve at the muzzle end goes up (12 o'clock) or down (6 o'clock), rather than off to one side or the other. I have not done any accuracy testing on this, so I can't say for sure that it really makes any difference on accuracy, but indexing the muzzle to 12 o'clock definitely helps with long range shooting by giving a few more minutes of useable scope elevation. If your scope has limited windage adjustment and you have the curve off to one side, you sometimes run out of windage adjustment on your scope before you get it sighted in. The bore curvature isn't always a straight curve, but can be a compound curve where it curves up and slightly to the side also. But this does not seem to matter at all, so I just index the action to make the bore point up or down at the muzzle, never to the side.

Bore at muzzle end indexed/clocked "up" for long range shooting. This also helps to minimize problems keeping optics within their normal adjustment range, especially with scopes that have limited built-in windage adjustment

Reamers: It is simplest to use a chamber reamer that already has the desired neck diameter and throat length built into it, which is what most gunsmiths use, but then you are stuck with whatever that reamer's dimensions are. I greatly prefer more versatility than that, so I often use a separate neck and/or throat reamer after cutting the initial chamber. I always get my match chamber reamers made with a tight neck and a short throat. I do the same with non-match reamers for chambers that different customers may want specific neck and/or throat dimensions in. I also often reduce the body dimensions slightly on match reamers to get a closer fit of the brass to the chamber than a SAAMI reamer does, which can help accuracy. *Be very careful to not reduce dimensions too much, which can cause cases to stick in the chamber and raise pressures!*

After I have reamed the chamber, I have the option of leaving the chamber as-is with a tight neck and/or short throat, or I can change the neck and throat as needed. I can use a separate neck reamer for a no-turn neck if the customer does not want to turn case necks, and/or I can use a separate throating reamer to match a particular bullet or seating depth the customer wants to use. It does take a little more work and skill to chamber a barrel this way, but I have chambered this way for most of my gunsmithing career and it works wonderfully well for getting barrels chambered and throated exactly the way many different customers want things!

The chamber reamer is cartridge-specific, but I only need one throat reamer per bore size (22, 6mm, 6.5mm, etc) and one or maybe two neck reamers per bore size to do all the cartridges in that bore size. This versatility saves from having to buy a separate chamber reamer for every neck and throat variation of every cartridge that different customers want, which would be extremely expensive – or, a lot of your customers will have to compromise and make do with whatever reamer options you do have.

I have used a micrometer-adjustable reamer stop (MARS II) on my standard throat reamers, and it also works great on my neck and chamber reamers. It is a great tool for controlling your headspace and throat depths precisely while chambering. (This MARS II tool is available from www.CustomGunsandAmmunition.com - Nat Lambeth). But other than that, my favorite throaters are Uni-Throaters from PTG, which are fully adjustable for setting the freebore of a throat exactly where you want it, and will cut a perfectly smooth, chatter-free throat if used in the correct barrels.

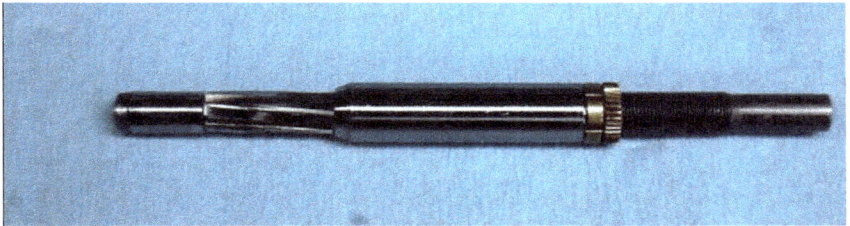

This is a 5-flute spiral Uni-Throater from Pacific Tool and Gauge for throating 5R-type barrels – after testing I prefer straight vs spiral reamers on 5R barrels

To minimize the throat reamer from developing chatter, I use 5-flute Uni-throaters for 5R barrels, and standard 6-flute Uni-Throaters for any barrel with conventional rifling, no matter how many lands and grooves. Sometimes if the throater really wants to develop some chatter, I have found it can work very well to switch back and forth between the 5-flute and 6-flute throaters during the throating process. I am still continually testing and trying to come up with better methods for dealing with reamer chatter in 5R barrels, but so far this is what I have found to work the best for me.

One thing I am adamant about is carefully inspecting every chamber, and especially every throat, with my Hawkeye borescope after it's finished. I commonly see large rough burrs on the side edges of the lands in factory throats (see photos below), but every once in a while in my own chambers I find a small wire-edge/burr has developed on the trailing side of each land where the throat has been cut, which is not good. This usually means the reamer is getting some chip-weld built up on the cutting edges, or it is getting dull, even if it seems like its cutting OK. Whenever I see this, I know it's time to send the reamer out to be re-sharpened.

These next two photos each show one land in the throat of factory barrels – barrel is pointing up with the chamber just below the photos, and the freebore part of the throat is at bottom of photos

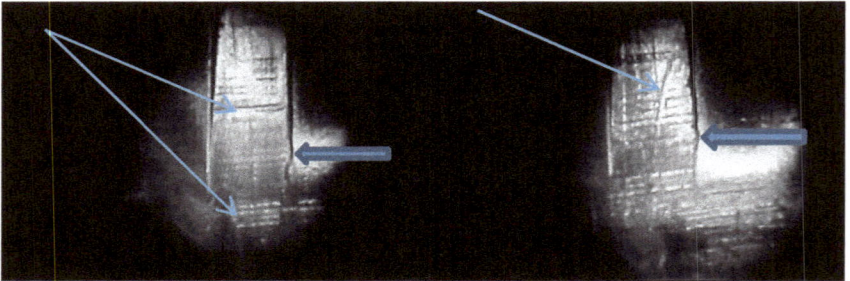

Burr is visible as a ragged edge along right side of land in this factory barrel's throat. Throat also has deep cross-scratches most likely from chip-weld on the reamer

Burr is visible as ragged edge along right side of land in this throat. There is also a cleaning rod gouge running at an angle up the face of the land in this throat

Whenever I find burrs in a throat, I need to deal with them now, since they will damage the bullet when it's going past, which will hurt accuracy. No, these burrs won't quickly shoot out, just like burrs on a crown won't quickly shoot out, even after hundreds of rounds in most cases, so you need to deal with this if you want top accuracy out of the barrel. I can often simply throat forward slightly with a separate throating reamer, but only if it won't hurt to have a slightly longer throat. If this is not an option, I can remove the burrs by hand-lapping the bore, especially the throat area, with abrasive on a cast-lead lap. This does have to be done correctly or you can damage the barrel, but I have done this for many years even on chambered and finished barrels and it works great! I do teach how to hand-lap barrels in my classes and am making an instructional DVD on the proper way to do this, but I do not have the space to go into detail on it here.

Minimizing/Eliminating Reamer Chatter: Gunsmiths can occasionally run into a problem when chambering barrels where the reamer starts to chatter and does not cut a nice smooth chamber. Contrary to what so many "experts" on the internet forums say, the reamer itself is usually not the problem here (other than a too-loose pilot or bushing fit in the bore), so don't right away blame the reamer or the reamer maker. It does help to minimize or prevent chatter by holding the reamer solidly in a fixed holder or tailstock chuck during the first ½ to ¾ of the chamber, then switch to your reamer holder to finish the chamber.

Chatter often starts right at the beginning of the chambering process by a sharp reamer digging into one side when it first touches one side of the chamber hole, then bouncing to the other side to dig in there, and it's chattering from then on. It rarely comes out of it on its own and usually gets worse, sometimes much worse. It is also very common be running completely chatter-free through the first ¾ or so of the chamber, then suddenly start to develop some chatter as soon as the throat starts to cut.

I frequently see chatter to one degree or another, almost always when chambering the currently popular 5R (also called 5C/canted-land/ramped-land) type barrels. Keep a close eye on when the chamber reamer has advanced far enough in to start cutting the throat. When it does, stop and clean all the oil and chips out of the chamber, then use your long-reach indicator to carefully indicate the freebore section of the throat, the neck, and the chamber body to make sure it is cutting smooth and round. If the indicator needle now is not staying smooth, but jumps slightly a number of times (usually 5) per barrel revolution, this means you are experiencing reamer chatter, and will want to do something about it before you finish chambering this barrel, unless it stays very minor.

I started seeing this unexpected reamer chatter phenomenon as soon as I started using 5R/5C-type barrels quite a few years ago. I called the barrel maker about it a number of times, but he told me he had checked with a number of other top gunsmiths around the country who used his barrels, and that I was the only gunsmith he knew of who was seeing this. I told him maybe I was the only guy who consistently measures for this all the way through the chambering process. I still see it to this day on almost every 5R barrel I chamber when using standard chambering reamers.

I can almost always predict exactly when the chatter will start in a 5R barrel. I will be chambering along and every time I check, the indicator shows absolutely no chatter whatsoever anywhere in the chamber. But in almost every 5R barrel I do, as soon as the reamer is far enough in to where the throat just begins to cut, I will then instantly be able to measure chatter in the neck area, and it often extends through the whole length of the chamber.

Usually it's very minor at this point, and if you didn't measure for it you'd never know anything was going on unless it becomes severe, which it can easily do if you don't catch it in time. I've experimented and tested extensively over the years trying to figure out what causes this and how to control it. In my opinion, what happens is conventional-land barrels have straight vertical sides on the lands, so when the straight vertical flutes on the reamer cuts into them, they meet square and there is no side pressure on the reamer flutes so they cut very nicely with no chatter.

However, in 5R barrels the sides of the lands are sloped at an angle, so the flutes of the reamer want to ride up the angled/ramped sides of the lands instead of cutting straight into them. Most 5R-type barrels are an odd number like 5 land/groove, so each time a reamer flute cuts the ramped side of the land it's cutting, it rides up the side of the land which forces the opposing reamer flute to cut into the groove between the opposite lands - you can easily see this in a borescope if you know what to look for. When you indicate the freebore part of the throat with your indicator, you'll find that the throat is now 5-sided and not round!

If you don't catch it quickly or remove it as soon it starts to develop, the chatter can get away from you. It can easily become severe enough that the effective diameter of the freebore section of the throat is smaller than the reamer itself due to the partially remaining lands left by the chatter. The reamer just flexes up and down cutting deeper into the grooves and not quite removing all of the lands, which is the chatter that you are measuring with your indicator. I've seen and measured it several times where reamer chatter in the throat got away from someone badly enough that the effective freebore diameter was even smaller than the bullet diameter. In these barrels the bullet will not advance through the freebore up to the lands in the throat, causing accuracy and pressure issues. This makes for unhappy customers!

These next two drawings show the difference between conventional and 5R rifling being cut by a standard six-flute reamer. The solid lines in the barrels are the original lands and grooves in the barrel. The dashed lines around the bore depict the shape of the <u>freebore</u> part of the throat after chambering.

Conventional   5R

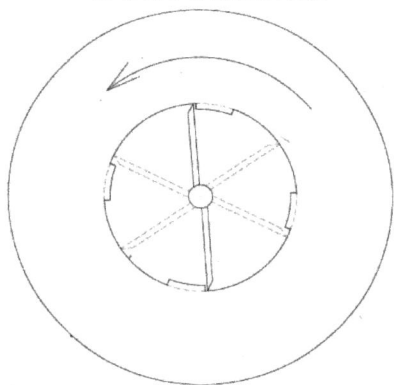

Drawing of a reamer cutting conventional rifling. Note that the reamer flutes meet the sides of the lands squarely, and the lands are cut away smoothly with no chatter

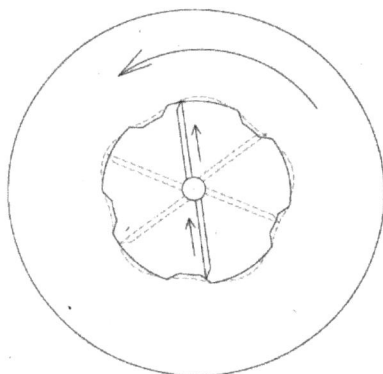

Drawing of a standard 6-flute reamer cutting 5R rifling. Note how reamer rides up sloped sides of lands and cuts into opposite groove. This deflection occurs every time a flute cuts a land, creating chatter in the throat. This chatter often extends through neck and entire chamber

I'm a huge believer in the value of using a borescope to inspect your work while chambering! Here are two borescope photos of a throat with no chatter, and then two more photos of a 5R throat with visible chatter. This is much easier to see and understand when you view it live in a borescope, since you can rotate the view to see much more than just these narrow screenshots. All these photos show the barrel oriented with the muzzle end up and the chamber end down.

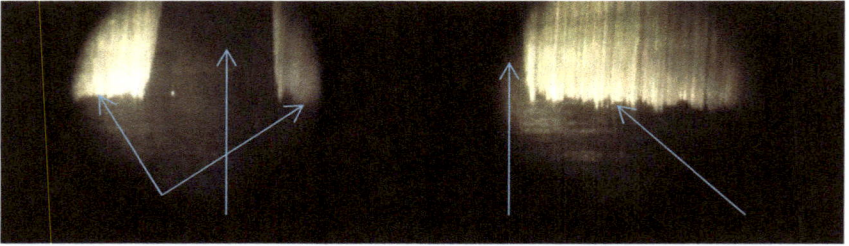

Throat with no chatter: land is in upper center, with freebore cut nice and straight across the land and the grooves on both sides of the land

Throat with no chatter: side of land is just visible on left – freebore in throat is cut straight across in the groove between the lands

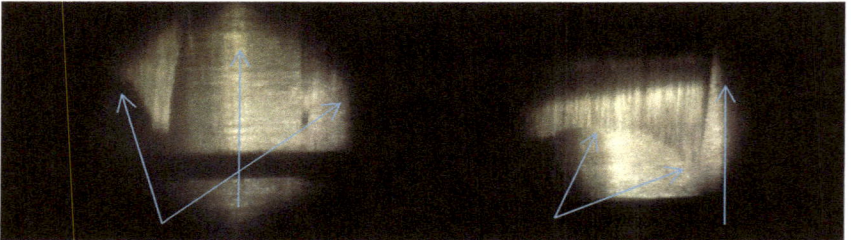

5R reamer chatter: end of neck is near bottom in this photo, land is in center with chatter in the grooves along both sides of land. Reamer did not cut land away in throat like it should, which can easily be measured with your long-reach dial indicator

5R reamer chatter: Land is on right, groove is on left – you can see where reamer has cut deeply into center of groove, but much shallower next to the land where the reamer has ridden up the land and away from the groove

One note here that I should make is that I'm not sure that a small amount of throat chatter in 5R barrels is such a bad thing, as long as it hasn't gotten away from you. If the chatter in the freebore section of the throat is minor enough that the effective diameter of the freebore is still slightly larger than bullet diameter, then the "lands" remaining in the freebore section formed by the chatter would act as a bullet guide to help center the bullets into the throat – a concept similar to "bore-rider" bullets or "bore-rider" throat shapes that some folks are testing and experimenting with.

5R barrels do seem to shoot very well most of the time, but at this time I'm not sure if they are just a current fad, or if they actually offer any advantage over conventional rifling, other than possibly a slight velocity increase. I chamber a lot of both types and can't say that I've seen any accuracy difference at all between them. I do know they are much more prone to reamer chatter than barrels with conventional rifling, so it always takes me longer to chamber one.

It's amazing how much a reamer will flex when cutting the lands while chambering, and it's especially prone to do this in 5R-type barrels (it can do it in conventional land barrels also, but not nearly so readily). It can flex and produce chatter no matter how true you have the bore dialed in, how well-fitted the reamer bushing is in the bore, how carefully you feed the reamer in, what type of cutting oil you use, or how big and expensive your lathe is.

Carbide reamers are much stiffer and won't chatter as bad, but most conventional chambering and throating reamers are HSS (high speed steel), which can chatter very easily in 5R barrels.

There are several things you can do to minimize or eliminate this issue. One thing I've found is to use 5-flute reamers if the barrels have 5 lands and grooves (5R, 5C, etc). You can also use carbide reamers, which will generally work very well. But I have developed another method to deal with this that works quite well when you use a standard 6-flute HSS reamer in a 5R barrel.

After pre-drilling and boring the chamber hole true, simply go forward into the bore and bore the lands away ahead of the chamber hole nearly to the end of where the neck will end up. Another variation of this I'm experimenting with that seems to work well is to use a 5-flute throating reamer to cut the lands away to just short of where the finished throat will end (measure very carefully so you don't cut too far forward). These methods allow the chamber reamer to advance much further into the chamber and become more fully supported by the neck and body of the chamber, before the throat portion of the reamer finally starts to cut as it nears the end of the chambering process.

A reamer that is more fully supported by walls of the chamber it is cutting cannot flex as easily as a partially supported reamer, which really helps to minimize chatter problems caused by the ramped 5R lands. It also helps as soon as the throat starts to cut, to greatly reduce the feed-rate (feed the reamer into the chamber much slower) when cutting the last portion of a 5R chamber.

When you do find chatter starting to develop, especially in the body of the chamber, you can normally remove the chatter quite easily by cutting a small slit in the center of a smaller (1" - 1 ¼") cleaning patch and sliding it over the nose of the reamer up to the shoulder. You can also cut a small piece of wax paper to wrap around the reamer. I especially use wax paper if I have to deal with chatter when getting near the end of the chamber to make sure it won't cut oversize.

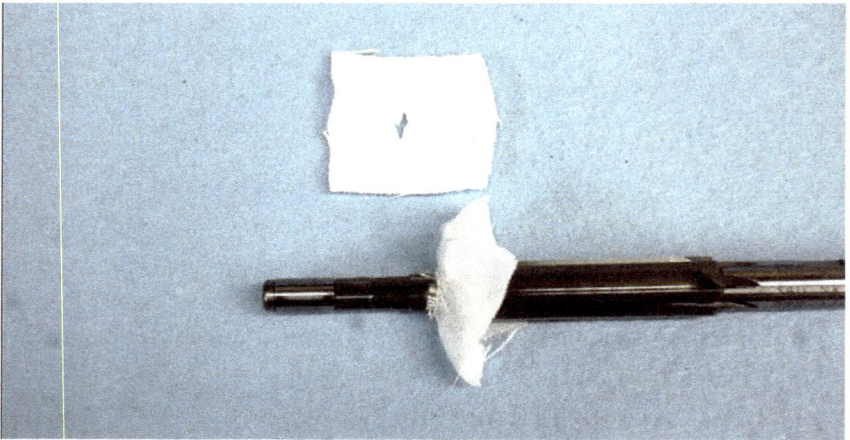

Remove chatter from the chamber by using a slit cleaning patch over the nose of the reamer. Oil the reamer and advance reamer into the rotating chamber carefully. As soon as you can feel that it has cut through the patch and started cutting metal, stop and check – almost always the chatter will now be gone

To do this, oil the reamer and patch/wax paper, start the lathe, and advance the reamer into the chamber until you can feel it just start to cut. One of the reamer flutes will cut through first, the patch/wax paper will dampen the reamer flex/vibrations, and usually the one flute that first cuts through the patch or wax paper will instantly remove the chatter. If the chatter has become rather severe before you caught it, it may take two or three passes with the patch or wax paper to remove it completely. It works best to stop cutting as soon as you feel the first flute cut through, clean and re-indicate the chamber to see if any chatter remains, then repeat as necessary until the chatter is gone.

Once the initial chamber is completed, if you have to cut a longer throat in a 5R barrel with a separate throating reamer, you really have to be extra careful the chatter doesn't get away from you if using anything other than a 5-flute throater. You want to cut slowly and carefully with any throater in a 5R barrel, since the body of the throater is completely unsupported and will very easily flex while riding up the angled lands, and it can chatter badly.

It is very difficult to use wax paper on a throater to keep the chatter down, so I have recently switched to 5-flute throaters on 5R barrels, and sometimes even a combination of switching 5-flute and 6-flute throaters back and forth during the throating process will work well. This will usually remove any excess chatter that may have developed in the throat area, and helps to throat forward much smoother, making these 5R barrels easier to deal with.

Reaming the chamber neck larger is a pretty straight-forward reaming operation. It can be very difficult to feel the neck reamer cutting, so it's hard to know when to stop without cutting too far. I find it really helps to use my borescope when reaming a larger neck, since then I can easily see how much I have left to cut.

Now we will go through the process of chambering a barrel from start to finish. In this next section, I will first give a quick, basic step-by-step overview of the chambering process. Then I will take you through the entire chambering process again, with every step explained in much greater detail.

Chambering - Basic Overview:

1. Make sure all action work is done and bolt lugs are lapped prior to starting barrel work. Remember to open/enlarge hole in recoil lug, if needed, after truing action threads.

2. Slug/evaluate barrel to make sure barrel is good, and that twist rate is correct. Determine where end(s) of barrel need to be cut off (make sure to check where it will fit in stock inletting if it's a sporter contour to help determine where to cut chamber end).

3. Measure action to determine tenon/thread dimensions, including fitting the bolt nose (I typically leave around .008" for all clearances, but note that some actions may vary considerably from this).

4. Measure reamer OD at body/shoulder junction, and the cartridge body length to determine size and depth to pre-drill for chamber.

5. Make "dimension card" writing down all dimensions needed to fit and chamber this barrel.

6. Load barrel in lathe – initially dial bore to within .001" to .002" at chamber end, and within .005" on outboard end.

7. Pre-drill chamber - use drill bit at least .030" smaller than shoulder OD. Drill to depth about .100" to .150" shorter than cartridge body (.200" short on 5R-type barrels will be good). Remember to allow for any cartridge protrusion on barrels with no bolt recess or shallow cone breech.

8. Finish dialing in bore so the 1.5" to 2" section of bore ahead of chamber is straight and true to within .0001" to .0002".

9. Now that the bore ahead of the chamber is dialed-in and running perfectly true, true the pre-drilled chamber hole with a boring bar. This ensures that the chamber, and the beginning section of bore directly ahead of the chamber, are aligned perfectly straight and true to each other, and also to the lathe.

10. If doing a 5R or canted-land barrel, use a small boring bar to bore the lands away ahead of the chamber hole to just short of

where the finished neck will end. Removing the lands here will minimize the angled lands causing reamer to chatter.

11. Cut tenon to length and diameter. It's OK to leave it a bit long now – you will cut it to exact final length later after indexing.

12. Thread it to fit the action. It's good to make threads slightly looser on untrued factory actions to make sure you get a good shoulder joint.

13. Use Prussian Blue or inletting black to make sure barrel/action shoulder joint is good.

14. Mark high side of muzzle, then cut shoulder forward to index/clock action until muzzle end of barrel indexes "up" for long range guns, and "up" or "down" for short range guns (mainly not to side in any gun).

15. Cut tenon to final finish length - leave tenon length .008" short for bolt nose end-play clearance on most types of actions.

16. Fit bolt nose to barrel – leave around .008" end play between bolt & barrel. Leave .008" side clearance in Rem-style bolt nose recess in most cases (.010" to .012" for untrued factory actions).

17. Chamber barrel - slow rpm and <u>very slow infeed</u> at first to keep reamer from chattering. Check after first .050" or so!! If chatter is present, simply bore the chattered section back to true, and try again.

18. If chatter starts to develop part-way through the chambering process, use slit patch over reamer nose (or wax paper wrapped around it) to remove chatter. This can make chamber slightly oversize, so if possible don't do this way at the end of process.

19. I take longer cuts at first, but I pull reamer out and clean off chips every 025" once the shoulder starts to cut. Any farther than this, you take a chance on the chips building up enough in the reamer flutes to score and cut rings in the chamber.

20. When getting to last .025" to .050" from the end, use a 1981 or older penny to remove minor chip weld and lightly dress reamer edges to help get good smooth throat, shoulder, and

chamber surfaces. Speed up rpm at the end to help get a better finish - 200 or more rpm is good.

21. Finish chamber to set the following <u>minimum</u> headspace specs in lathe with action hand-tight - this will get headspace near-zero later when torqued on:

> .0005"-.001" on good custom actions w/o recoil lug
>
> .001"-.0015" on custom actions w/ recoil lug or trued factory actions w/o recoil lug
>
> .0015" for trued factory actions w/ recoil lug
>
> .002"-.0025" for untrue factory actions w/ or w/o recoil lug

22. CRITICAL FINAL SAFETY DOUBLE-CHECKS: Gauge headspace with both Go and .002" No-Go gauges. Also make sure cartridge case goes into chamber all the way to the extractor groove so it is completely supported by chamber!

23. Cut larger diameter neck in chamber, if needed.

24. Throat for longer bullets if needed.

25. Lightly chamfer edge of chamber and edge of bolt nose recess (not needed on cone-breech chambers). Polish chamber with no smoother than 320 grit sandpaper and oil. Polish/radius chamber mouth with sandpaper/oil also.

26. Remove barrel from lathe. Install/tighten action to about 100 ft/lb torque, then gauge to double-check and make sure finished headspace is good.

27. Then remove barrel from action, stamp/engrave caliber on barrel, and polish/finish outside of barrel (I do this before crowning since I use a barrel spinner to polish barrel, and will not put the center of a barrel spinner in a finished crown).

28. Finally, load barrel back into lathe, dial it in, crown barrel, and install muzzle brake or tuner, if needed.

29. Remove barrel from lathe, install it in action, assemble gun, double-check headspace and bolt lug contact, and it is now ready to test-fire.

CHAMBERING: Detailed Step-by-Step

1. Measure the action to determine tenon/thread dimensions – including fitting the bolt nose. I prefer to leave around .008" for all clearances between the bolt nose and barrel in most actions, but some types of actions will require more.

2. Measure reamer OD at the shoulder, and the cartridge body length to determine size and depth to pre-drill for chamber.

3. Load barrel in headstock of lathe. It will save time to start out by holding the chamber end of the barrel against a live center, and get the outboard end visually close to center while setting the outboard screws against the barrel. Support barrel with shims under outboard screws and on the working end with shims under the front 1/8" to 1/4" of the chuck jaws. If possible, let barrel protrude from chuck 2" to 3" so the chamber is not compressed under the jaws.

This photo shows the barrel set up for the "through the headstock" chambering method

4. Start by initially dialing the bore to .001" to .002" at the chamber end, and within .005" on the outboard end. This gets the bore straight enough to pre-drill the chamber, and if you're using a range rod, it lets the bushing slide back and forth without binding and damaging the bore. Note that I <u>always</u> radius and polish the leading edges of all my reamer/range rod bushings, so they slide in the bore without scraping and damaging the tops of the lands.

Leading edges of the reamer bushing on the range rod are radiused and polished so it will slide back and forth very smoothly in the bore without scraping and damaging the tops of the lands

5. Pre-drill the chamber - use a drill bit at least .030" smaller than shoulder OD. Drill to depth about .100" to .150" shorter than cartridge body (.200" on 5R-type barrels so reamer will become fully supported sooner in the process to minimize chatter). Don't drill too deep - remember to allow for the amount of cartridge head protrusion from the finished chamber, since the protrusion will be different depending on if it's a recessed Remington-style breech, a flat breech with no bolt nose recess, or a cone breech.

Pre-drilling the chamber with a twist drill to remove metal for dialing-in and more accurate chambering

6. Now if you are direct reading in the grooves with your long-reach indicator or using a range rod, finish dialing in the 1.5" to 2" section of bore just ahead of the pre-drilled chamber hole, getting this section running straight and true to within .0001" to .0002". (Note that for ease of instructions I call this area the "throat", when in reality it will actually be the neck/throat area). Once the bore ahead of the chamber is dialed in straight and true for a couple inches or so, having the actual throat area being the one spot to get true is not at all critical, since this whole section of barrel will be running straight and true to the lathe. So just know when I say throat during the dialing-in instructions, I am referring to the beginning part of the bore just ahead of the drilled chamber hole.

7. **Dialing-in process**: this is much more difficult to try to explain than it is to do once you've done it a few times. It goes like this:

a. I found while teaching my classes that almost everyone tightens the chuck jaws way too much trying to force things into alignment too aggressively during the dialing-in process. Being aggressive like that causes way too much "chasing", which is very time-consuming and frustrating. <u>I really stress to "finesse" all your adjustments until the barrel is dialed-in - don't force anything!</u> It will save much time re-dialing the barrel to zero each time if you only use very light tension on the chuck jaws and outboard spider screws during the entire dialing-in process. Then, after it is dialed-in using light tension, you will tighten the jaws and spider screws enough to hold the barrel for machining.

Number the chuck jaws and outboard spider screws on your lathe so you can keep track of adjustments while dialing-in barrels – eliminates "chasing" and speeds up the process

b. It saves time whenever you tighten or loosen the chuck jaws during the dialing-in process, to try to only let the indicator needle move one or two marks on the dial at a time so it doesn't get far from zero – this will keep you from chasing your adjustments too much. It really helps to permanently number your chuck jaws and spider screws to make it easy to keep track of adjustments, which also helps to keep from chasing.

c. Insert the indicator tip into the bore as far forward as it will go (usually about 1.5" ahead of the chamber if the chamber is large enough to allow the body of the indicator to go in) - or if using a range rod, you can go 2" ahead of the pre-drilled hole with the rod bushing – this is your "zero point". Depending on the cartridge and how far the barrel protrudes from the chuck, this "zero point" will normally be close to where the barrel is supported in the chuck. Roll the chuck/barrel by hand and adjust the bore run-out to zero at this point with the chuck.

Note that the front of the drilled chamber hole will usually be 1" or more outside the chuck jaws for most chambers, so having the "zero point" be 1.5"or 2" ahead of chamber works well. At other times you may have to chuck a barrel short or above the chamber, so if the front of the chamber is closer to being under the chuck jaw shims, it may work better to reverse these "zero and adjust" points in the instructions by making the "zero point" be the rearmost part of the bore, and the "adjusting point" be forward of the "zero point" – either way will work fine.

So, on any setup, just figure from your setup and the cartridge body length where the rear "zero point" will be, and dial accordingly to where this is in relation to the chuck/shim pivot point. *As an example here: I chamber a lot of short and medium length cartridges and usually have the barrel protruding 2.5" to 3" from the chuck, so I normally have my zero point 1.5" to 2" ahead of the chamber*, and have written these instructions for doing it that way.

Insert tip of the long-reach indicator as far into bore ahead of the chamber as possible – this is your "zero point". The tip of the indicator will be in the bore near to where the chuck jaws are holding the barrel. Use the chuck jaws to dial the bore run-out to zero at this point.

Now pull indicator tip back to just ahead of pre-drilled chamber – this is your "adjust point". If there is run-out at this point, make an outboard spider adjustment. Follow instructions to go back and forth dialing to zero with chuck and making outboard spider adjustments until this section of bore is dialed in straight and true

d. Pull the indicator tip or range rod back 1.5" or 2" to what I call the "adjust point", making sure it does not come back into the drilled chamber hole. The indicator tip or range rod bushing should now be behind the chuck jaw "pivot point" in most chambers if the barrel is protruding 2" to 3" from the chuck.

95

Roll the barrel and find the low side of run-out in this end of the bore. If the indicator is reading low here, and the chuck jaws forward of this are the "pivot point" (basically zero here), this means the barrel will be high on the outboard end of the lathe.

e. Now make a small outboard adjustment by loosening the bottom screw and tightening the top screw on your outboard "spider" to push the outboard end of the barrel down. The barrel will pivot at the chuck jaws and bring the chamber end of the barrel up. In most cases don't try to "dial" the barrel to a particular indicator reading when making an outboard end adjustment, since the distance from the chuck jaw pivot point to the actual barrel "zero point" will vary in every barrel, plus the barrel will be bending slightly from this outboard adjustment. You won't get accurate readings and will just find yourself chasing too much, which will really slow you down.

f. Go back to the chuck end and move indicator tip or range rod forward in barrel 1.5" or 2" – back to your original "zero point".

g. **It is very important to relax the barrel from the slight bend induced by the outboard adjustment you just made.** Slowly loosen all 4 chuck jaws incrementally until the tension is off the jaws. It will save time by not letting the indicator needle move more than a mark or two at a time as you loosen it - staying close to your zero prevents "chasing" so much.

h. Now tighten chuck jaws <u>lightly</u> and dial bore to zero again.

i. Pull indicator tip back 1.5" to the "adjust point", roll barrel, and see if any run-out remains after your last adjustment.

j. If so, put the "adjust point" low side down, do the outboard adjustment again to push the outboard end down, which will raise the "adjust point" up.

k. Then go back to the chuck side, move indicator tip forward to the "zero point" - loosen/relax barrel, and re-zero.

l. Pull indicator tip back to "adjust point" - see if run-out remains.

m. Repeat steps f. through k. as often as needed until the bore is dialed-in and reads zero or near-zero all the way through the "throat to 1.5" to 2" forward" section you are dialing-in.

n. Now that you're dialed in, you must snug the outboard spider screws enough that they won't work loose (not real tight since this end is just supporting the barrel), then tighten the chuck jaws incrementally until they are tight enough to hold the barrel for machining. After you've tightened everything up, make sure the bore is dialed as close to zero as possible in the throat area.

o. Now double-check your work - measure forward and back with the indicator/range rod to make sure the barrel is still running straight and true through this whole 1.5" to 2" section of bore.

p. Note that if the barrel came out of true/straightness after tightening up the chuck jaws, this usually is an indication that your chuck jaw shims are compressing unevenly, and are not perfectly opposing each other on opposite sides of the barrel, causing a "scissors effect", if you will, forcing a bend into the barrel – not good! Whenever I get this, or if the barrel seems extra difficult to get dialed-in, I check my chuck jaw shims and replace them if necessary, so the barrel does not bend when I tighten the chuck jaws. This does happen fairly often, so I just want you to know what to do when it happens.

q. When crowning the barrel later, just repeat this same process to get the bore dialed-in straight and true at the muzzle end.

8. Now that the beginning part of the bore just ahead of the chamber is dialed-in, you must true the pre-drilled chamber hole

with a boring bar so it also runs true. Now the entire chamber, plus the beginning section of bore directly ahead of the chamber, are aligned together as a unit and running straight and true.

After the bore ahead of the chamber is dialed-in, use a small carbide boring bar to true the pre-drilled chamber hole, so it will now be in perfect alignment to the beginning section of the bore

9. If doing a 5R-type barrel, I take an extra step here to minimize reamer chatter. Bore the lands away ahead of the pre-drilled chamber just deep enough to cut the lands away and get at least .002" or so into the grooves. Don't worry, the necks of your brass

Preparing to bore the lands away ahead of the pre-drilled chamber in a 5R barrel. Set the length of the boring bar to end at least .050" short of the end of the neck on the cartridge – this way you cannot bore too far forward

Reaching way in with a boring bar to bore the lands away at the beginning of the bore just ahead of the pre-drilled chamber in a 5R barrel

cartridge cases are way thicker than .002", so you're fine. Go far enough forward into the bore so the lands are removed to about .050" or so short of where the finished neck will end. Make at least three cleanup passes with the boring bar, then check with your indicator to make sure the lands are really gone and the hole is round. Boring the lands away here will minimize the angled lands' tendency to cause the reamer to flex and chatter.

10. Cut the tenon to length and diameter. It's OK to leave it a few thousandths long now since you will cut it to final length later after indexing/clocking the action.

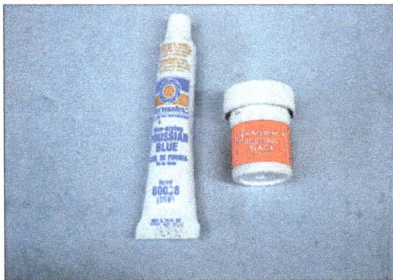

Use inletting black or Prussian Blue to check your barrel to action joint

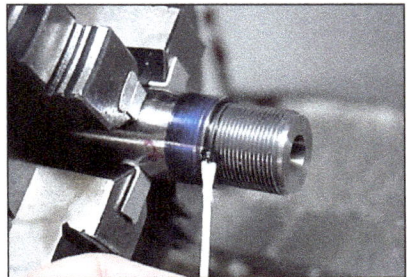

Apply a thin even layer of inletting black to spinning barrel shoulder with a Q-tip. When using a recoil lug between action and barrel, put a thin layer on action face also

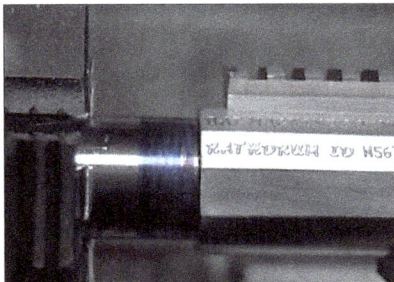

Screw action against shoulder - the inletting black will transfer from the barrel shoulder to the action face anywhere it touches. If using a recoil lug, the inletting black on barrel shoulder and on action face will get transferred to anywhere that it touches the lug

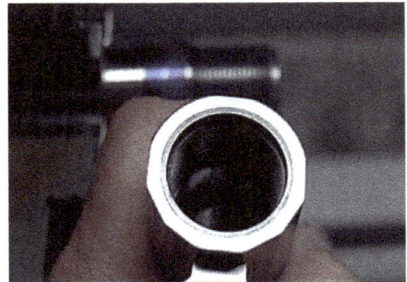

Inletting black has transferred from barrel shoulder to action face – this joint shows perfect contact all the way around, which is what you want!

11. **Thread barrel to fit the action**. Use Prussian Blue or inletting black to make sure barrel/action shoulder joint is good. You will probably need to cut the threads slightly looser to get a good shoulder joint when fitting a barrel to an untrued factory action.

12. Mark the high side of barrel at the muzzle. Then cut the shoulder forward enough to index/clock action so the high side indexes "up" for long range guns, and "up" or "down" for short range guns (never to the side in any gun).

Checking for high side of muzzle end run-out after dialing-in bore at the chamber end. If bore is near-center in the barrel, you can simply indicate on the outside of the barrel like I'm doing here, but if bore is off-center more than a few thousandths, then you should indicate in the bore

Machine enough material from the shoulder so the action screws on farther – go until the action aligns so the bore curvature is up or down at the muzzle end

Use a dial indicator against carriage to tell exactly how far forward you are machining the shoulder

Now the action screws on far enough so top of action is aligned to where I marked the bore curvature

13. Cut tenon to final finish length - make tenon length to leave around .008" bolt nose end-play clearance in most actions.

14. Fit bolt nose to barrel, leaving around .008" end play between bolt and barrel in most actions, and .008" side clearance in Rem-style bolt nose recess in most cases (.010" to .012" for untrued actions). Note some actions require more clearance than this, but no actions should be less than .005" anywhere when assembled.

15. **Chamber the barrel**. Don't worry if your reamer bushing isn't in the bore yet on longer chambers – it will follow the pre-drilled/trued hole perfectly and track dead-center into the bore when it gets there. I've chambered thousands of barrels and over half of them the bushing didn't get to the bore until the reamer had gone in a ways. I rarely use a floating reamer holder since the tailstock of my lathe aligns perfectly to the headstock, which helps.

If you find your reamer wants to chatter when using a floating reamer holder, it may help to not use the floating holder at first until the bushing gets to the bore. It works great to use a fixed reamer holder or even a tailstock drill chuck for the first ½ to ¾ of the chamber, then switch to a floating reamer holder to finish it.

16. ***Important - measure for chatter or runout after your first cut of .050" or so!*** No matter which type of reamer holder you use, it helps to use slow rpm and <u>very</u> slow in-feed initially to keep the reamer from chattering when it very first starts to cut – it can do so quite easily on this first cut. If any chatter is present, you can simply bore it back true with a boring bar, or use a patch or wax paper on the reamer to remove the chatter, and then try again.

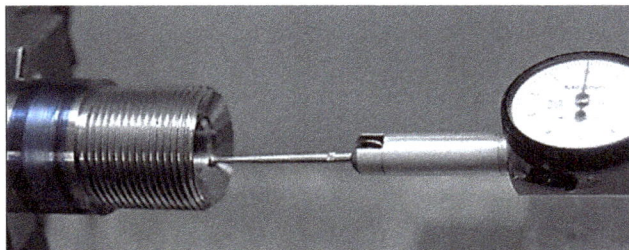

Measure for chatter or run-out after making first chambering cut

17. It can help to smooth the cutting edges on the reamer by "stropping" or rubbing the cutting edges lightly with a 1981 or older copper penny, especially if this is a new reamer with super-sharp edges that can tend to dig in and chatter on the first cut.

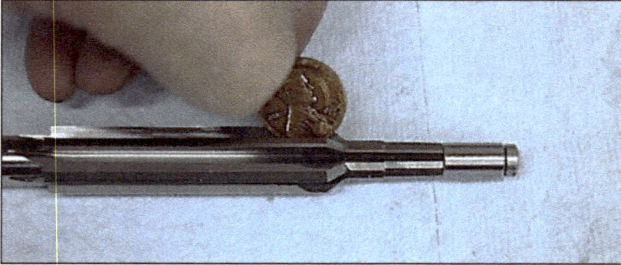

Using a penny to help remove chip-weld and lightly smooth cutting edges of reamer

18. I feel it is absolutely critical to check for runout, chatter, or any other possible problems, by dial-indicating the chamber every .250" or so throughout the entire chambering process, and every .100" or so in 5R barrels after the throat has started cutting.

Measure for chatter and run-out every .250" through the entire chambering process

The issue is not _if_ a problem may develop during the chambering process, but _when_! You will find this out if you start checking every chamber. You really want to detect any problems that may develop as early as possible, so you can deal with it immediately while you still can - and definitely before it gets away from you!

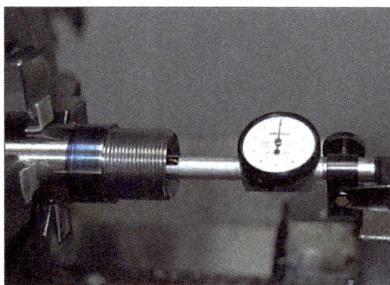

Once throat has started to cut in 5R-type barrels, measure for chatter every .100" until done – measure in body of chamber, and especially in the neck and in the freebore part of the throat

Now with the chamber nearly finished, everything is still running true, with zero run-out through chamber, throat, as well as into the bore well ahead of the throat

19. If chatter starts to develop part-way through the chambering process, slit a small patch and slide it over the reamer nose up to the shoulder (or wrap wax paper around the forward half of the reamer). The patch works great but can make the chamber cut slightly oversize, so try not to use a patch near the end of the chambering process – best to use wax paper if in last .250" or so.

20. When getting to the last .025" or so of the chamber, use an old copper penny to remove minor chip-weld and lightly dress the reamer edges to help get a good smooth throat, shoulder, and chamber finish. You may need to stone off the flat face of the reamer flutes, but make sure to not touch the cutting edge with a stone. If you've been chambering at a slower rpm until now, it will help to get a better throat finish to run at least 200 rpm or more for the last .025" to .050" of the chamber.

21. Use a Go headspace gauge in the chamber once the shoulder is getting cut by the reamer, so you'll know when you are nearing the correct depth. When you get close, it works very well to screw the action (with the bolt closed) against the Go gauge in the chamber, then use a feeler gauge to measure the gap between the barrel shoulder and the action to tell almost exactly how far you have to go yet to get to the proper chamber depth/headspace. You will have to chamber a little deeper than zero to account for how much "crush" you will get later when you torque the action onto the barrel in final assembly.

Use a feeler gauge to measure gap between action and barrel shoulder when nearing the end of the chamber

On actions with recoil lug, same thing - use a feeler gauge to measure gap between action and lug

22. I like to finish the chamber to end up with the following <u>minimum</u> "in-lathe" headspace with action hand-tight in the lathe:

.0005"-.001" on good custom actions w/o recoil lug

.001"-.0015" on custom actions w/ recoil lug or trued factory actions w/o recoil lug

.0015" for trued factory actions w/ recoil lug

.002"-.0025" for untrue factory actions w/ or w/o recoil lug

These "hand-tight" dimensions in the lathe will almost always allow headspace to end up between zero and .001" after you torque the barrel into the action during final assembly – perfect!

23. Check the headspace with a Go gauge, which should close with no feel at this point. You can then use a No-Go gauge to make sure you haven't gone too far. But most standard No-Go gauges are .004"-.005" longer than a Go gauge, which is too much to be useful in an accuracy chamber. You can special order No-Go gauges in .001" increments which is ideal, but quite costly.

24. I prefer to simply make a .002" No-Go gauge by adding a piece of .002" thick cellophane tape to the back of the Go gauge. This makes it into a .002" No-Go gauge, so it will be twice as accurate as a standard No-Go gauge. (Note that you can get cellophane tape in .0015" thickness also, giving even more accuracy and versatility).

The bolt should close with no feel on a Go gauge in your finished chamber, but should not close at all, or be snug on a .002" No-Go gauge. Then when you torque the action onto the barrel later after it is out of the lathe, you will end up with your headspace between zero and .001", which is ideal for accuracy!

Typical headspace Go gauge

You can make a .002" No-Go gauge by putting a layer of .002" thick cellophane tape on rear of Go gauge – very effective and much less expensive than custom No-Go gauges

25. Another way to check where the headspace is set while the barrel is in the lathe is by tightening the action hand-tight against the barrel shoulder with the Go gauge (no tape) in place. Close the bolt and place a .0001" indicator against the rear of the bolt. Push the bolt forward against the Go gauge, then pull it back against the lug seats to see how much forward and back movement there is, which is your "in-lathe headspace".

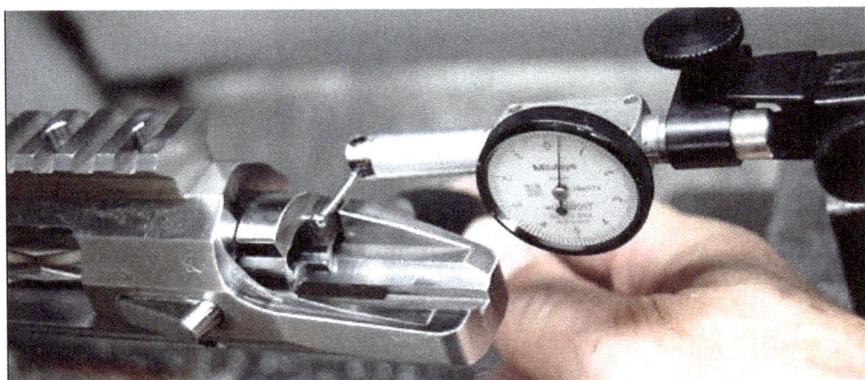

Using dial indicator on rear of bolt to measure "in-lathe" headspace

This works well with actions with tighter bolt fit, but does not work as well with looser factory actions since the extra side play of the sloppier bolt fit makes it hard to gauge the true amount of forward/back headspace movement.

But no matter what, even when measuring with a dial indicator, I still always physically double-check by making sure the bolt will close on a Go gauge, but will be tight or closes with some feel on a .002" No-Go gauge, just like I mentioned above.

26. ***Critically important!*** I really stress in my classes to always do a quick visual double-check when the chamber is completed to make sure for safety sake that the body of the chamber fully supports the cartridge case. So insert a cartridge or empty case, and no matter the type of barrel tenon (flat, coned, recessed Remington style, etc), the cartridge should go completely into the chamber up to the extractor groove. *If not, you've measured or done something wrong and now is the time to correct it!* I've twice seen this done wrong by other shops with disastrous results when their customer fired the first round.

***Always** visually double-check your measurements by seating a cartridge or piece of brass into the finished chamber to make sure the chamber fully supports the case body up to the extractor groove*

27. ***Important!*** Before continuing, double-check the chamber/bore run-out now to make sure you haven't made it come out-of-true when tightening and loosening the action while checking headspace. It is surprisingly easy when tightening/loosening the action in the lathe to bump the barrel a little out-of-true here since we aren't holding the barrel extremely tight in the chuck.

28. If needed, simply re-dial it to zero before going to the next step. Any redialing here almost always can be easily done with just some slight adjustment at the chuck end to bring the run-out back

to zero. Rarely do I have to do anything with the outboard spider screws at this point, since they primarily affect the straightness of the setup, and the chuck end mainly dials-in the rotational run-out.

29. **Neck Reaming**: Use a neck reamer to cut a larger diameter neck, if needed. Since I often get my chamber reamers made with a tight neck for more versatility, if the customer wants to turn necks on his brass, I can leave it as-is, but if he wants a no-turn neck, I now have the option to cut a larger diameter neck for him.

To do this, I use a neck reamer of the appropriate diameter. Put the neck reamer into your reamer holder, and gently slide it into the chamber until it comes close to the chamber neck. I then lock down the tailstock, and very carefully advance the reamer into the chamber until I feel the reamer stop up against the smaller chamber neck. I use a dial indicator on the tailstock and zero it at this point.

I need to know how long the chamber neck is, and can get this information from the reamer print, or even by measuring the length of the neck on the chamber reamer. I then start the lathe and advance in .100" increments to cut the new neck. You can just cut the new neck the appropriate amount, feeling for when it comes to the end of the original neck - but it can often be quite difficult to feel exactly when the reamer has come to the end of the neck. If you don't stop when you get to the end of the original neck, you will end up cutting into the freebore part of the throat, which isn't a huge problem, but nevertheless you really don't want to do that.

I prefer to stop about .025" to .050" short of the final depth, and use my borescope to double-check how much farther I have to go. This works very well, and when you see you are nearing the end, you can creep up to the end in .005" increments while using your borescope after each cut to make sure you stop just when you get to the end. You can also use a MARS II reamer stop on your reamer to set the correct depth of cut - this can be set to any depth desired in increments as small as .001".

Using a neck reamer to enlarge a tight-neck chamber to a no-turn neck

Here is a micrometer adjustable reamer stop (MARS II) set up on a neck reamer

The MARS II is set and the reamer is fed into the chamber until the stop touches the rear of the barrel- done!

30. **Throating**: Since I get most of my chamber reamers made with short throats for more versatility, this gives me the option of reaming a longer throat to set the optimum seating depth for any specific bullets my customer wants to shoot. Optimum throats for

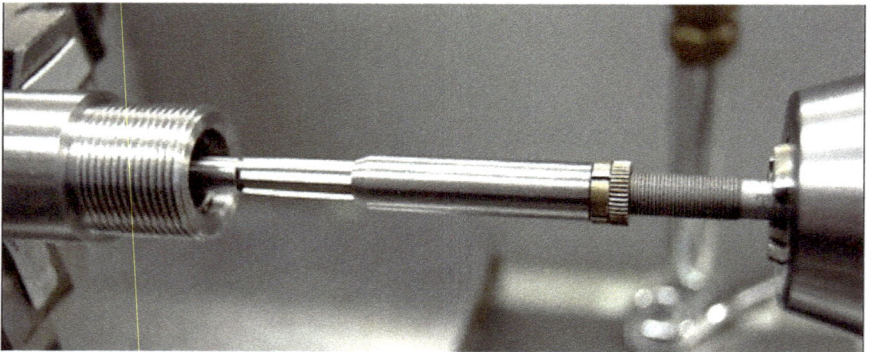

A PTG Uni-throater can be used to easily and accurately set the throat to be optimum for any bullet or dimensions the customer wants

hunting barrels are usually best with the bullets off the lands at least .040" to .050" to keep the pressures down and to make sure a bullet never sticks in the lands when extracting a loaded cartridge.

Competition and high-accuracy varmint shooters however often run the bullets into or extremely close to the lands, wherever the load development in a particular barrel shows it is best. Plus it is usually ideal to keep the bearing surface of the bullets ahead of the neck/shoulder junction - this keeps the bullets ahead of any donut that may form in the neck/shoulder junction of the brass after repeated firings. You can set the throat to account for all of this!

Throating reamers take such a light cut that it is extremely hard to tell when they are cutting, and consequently it is hard to know when you're at the correct throat length. It is so much easier to use a micrometer reamer stop like the MARS II units, or to use a PTG Uni-Throater, which is a throating reamer that can easily be set to stop exactly where you need the finished throat length to be.

31. Cut a light chamfer on the edge of the chamber to help cartridges feed in smoothly (not needed on cone-breech chambers). Polish the chamber lightly with no finer than 320 grit sandpaper and oil.

Use oil and 320 grit sandpaper on a split dowel to lightly polish chamber

Make sure to polish/radius the edge of the chamber mouth with sandpaper/oil to keep the brass from scraping when it is feeding in. Also, cut a light chamfer on the inner edge of a Remington-style bolt nose recess to make sure this does not bind on any radius where the front of the bolt lugs join the bolt body.

109

32. I think this next step is very important if you have a bore scope - *you do realize by now that it is huge advantage to use a borescope for extreme accuracy chambering, don't you!!!* ☺

Inspect the entire chamber, and especially the throat, with a bore scope to make sure there are no gouges or "rings" cut into the chamber. Even more important for accuracy is to inspect the throat to make sure the throat is as perfect and burr-free as possible. Really look at the lands in the throat to make sure there are no burrs on the edges of the lands caused by a dull reamer or by chip-weld built up on the reamer. This does affect accuracy, so if you find any issues at all, take care of them now while the barrel is still in the lathe and dialed-in.

If the lands have burrs on them, you can re-throat with a sharper or chip-weld-free throating reamer, or you can hand-lap the burrs from the throat. No matter what, make sure the throat is perfect!

33. Now the chamber is finished, it measures perfect, and looks great!

Finished chamber!

Inside of finished chamber!

34. Next, remove the barrel from the lathe, clean and grease the threads, and install/tighten the action to minimum 75-100 ft/lb torque for switch-barrel rifles and 150 ft/lb for hunting rifles. Then use Go and .002" No-Go gauges to double-check that the finished headspace is close to zero. Make sure the bolt will close on a loaded cartridge. It's a good idea to check feeding and function at this point also.

35. Remove barrel from the action, stamp/engrave caliber, then polish/finish barrel as desired.

36. Note that I always finish-polish the outside of the barrel in a barrel spinner before crowning, since the barrel spinner can easily damage a finished crown. I will then do any final finishing like bead-blasting, Cerakote®, or hot bluing after crowning the barrel.

37. **Crown**: For the crown, dial-in the muzzle end of the barrel with the same exact back and forth procedure that you dialed-in the chamber end. Machine a good crown by cutting from inside the bore toward the outside with an extremely sharp tool bit to eliminate burrs. I use 11 degrees most often, but the angle of the crown isn't nearly as important as getting the bore running true. I run my lathe at 770 rpm when cutting the crown, and use a cobalt HSS tool bit and sharpen it razor sharp before cutting each crown.

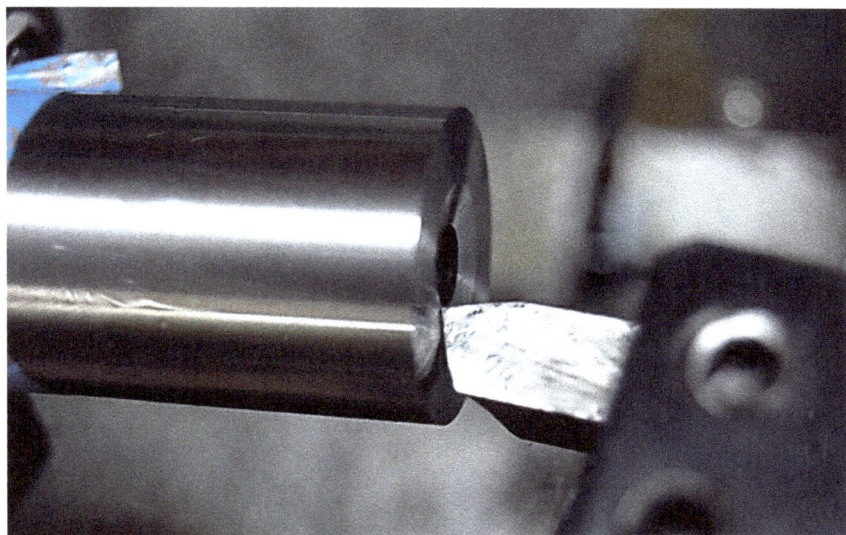

Cutting an 11 degree accuracy crown with a razor sharp HSS tool bit set at a very shallow angle - make sure to cut from the inside out to prevent burrs

After the crown is cut, I <u>always double-check</u> the dial-in of the bore with my .0001" dial indicator to make sure the bore is still running absolutely true. It almost always is still true, but it can and will come out of true on occasion, and you'll never know it if you don't check for it. So if it did come out of true while machining the crown, simply re-dial it in, and re-cut the crown again.

I know it does take extra time to do all the double-checking I do during the chambering and crowning processes, but this is important for accuracy, as well as to find and correct any issues that may arise along the way as early as possible, so I feel it is definitely worth the time it takes to do all this extra checking!

38. Once you have the crown cut, and you've verified that the bore is still running true, check the crown for burrs very carefully. Any burrs will damage the jackets of bullets as they go past, and will hurt accuracy!

I use a Q-Tip and drag it from the inside out all the way around, checking every land and groove. I also push a tight-fitting patch on a jag through the bore and out the muzzle with my cleaning rod. If I can see any hairs from the Q-Tip or patch, or if I feel the Q-Tip or patch drag at all going past the crown, this means there most likely are burrs on the sides of the lands at the crown. If so, I re-sharpen my crowning tool, and re-cut the crown again until it does come out smooth and burr-free.

While the barrel is still dialed in the lathe, you can bevel just the tips of the lands at a 45 degree angle with a razor sharp tool, or even with a Cratex abrasive tip shaped to a 45 degree cone.

I don't always so this on a crown, but when I do, I just break the tips of the lands and don't even usually get deep enough to cut into the grooves between the lands. This gives a little more crown protection by preventing the cleaning brushes and jags from dinging and wearing away the sharp ends of the lands so easily while cleaning the barrel. The cleaning rod and jags ride on top of the lands, so beveled edges on the lands don't get worn and dinged up as easily as sharp edges. Not mandatory at all, but it helps.

Cutting just the tips of the lands on the crown at a 45 degree angle – helps to see it better if you run the lathe in reverse with cutting tool at the back of the hole

Then I finish the crown by polishing the end of the muzzle up to the edge of the crown with oiled sandpaper while the barrel is spinning in the lathe, but make sure not to let the sandpaper get into the bore or you will likely damage the edge of the crown.

39. Install a muzzle brake or tuner, if needed, while the bore is still dialed-in true from crowning the barrel. I always bore the inside of a muzzle brake with a small boring bar after it is installed on the barrel to make sure the center hole of the brake aligns dead true to the centerline of the barrel bore. This will ensure there are no bullet strikes, but mostly I want the bullet to fly dead center through the center hole of the brake so escaping gases are exactly the same all the way around the bullet for best accuracy!

40. The barrel is now finished and ready to win matches, set records, or just ready for some extremely accurate shooting and hunting by a happy customer!! ☺

Specialty Tools for Chambering

Item numbers below are from MSC Industrial Supply 1-800-645-7270
www.mscdirect.com:

06249411   Mitotoyu #513-504 Dial Test Indicator Kit - this indicator comes with a .700" long point, and has a .375" diameter cylindrical body which will go into most chambers, and is the best indicator I have found for this method of extreme-accuracy chambering

06445464   1.500" long-reach indicator point with .080" diameter tip (I use this for 95% of my chambering) – note that this longer point reduces indicator values to around .0002" for each graduation

99046633   2.675" extra-long-reach indicator point - used when 1.500" point won't work, but reduces indicator values to around .0004" for each graduation

09560376   NOGA magnetic indicator holder (high quality)

05253000   Boring bar – works great for truing pre-drilled chamber holes

00101352   Boring bar " " (1/4" longer)

05253372   Boring bar " " (extra long for 30 cal magnums and larger – tip can be ground down for smaller bores)

08700023   Carmex external threading toolholder (use inserts below)

05765631   Inserts for cutting external threads (these indexable carbide tool bits work great for cutting threads in a manual lathe)

References

4D Reamer Rentals LTD, 432 E Idaho St., Suite C420, Kalispell, MT 59901
406-752-2520   www.4-dproducts.com

ARC Ballistics, Source for Reamers, Great Britain
http://www.arc-ballistics.com/

Brownells, Montezuma, IA 1-800-741-0015   www.brownells.com
Gunsmithing tools, parts, supplies

Clymer Manufacturing, Rochester Hills, MI, 248-853-5555
http://www.clymertool.com
Chamber Reamers and Headspace Gauges

Custom Guns and Ammunition/ MARS II ReamerStop Nat Lambeth,
Youngsville, NC 919-556-0554 www.customgunsandammunition.com
MARS II micro-adjustable reamer stop

Gradient Lens Corp, Rochester, NY 14608   1-800-536-0790
www.gradientlens.com *Hawkeye Borescopes*

GreTan/GTR Tooling, Rifle, CO 81650   970-878-5421
www.gretanrifles.com   *Reamer holders, action jig, etc*

Grizzly Industrial, 1-800-523-4777   www.grizzly.com *Gunsmith lathes, mills, tooling, etc*

Holland's Shooters Supply, Inc, Powers, OR   541-439-5155
www.hollandguns.com   *Tools, recoil lugs, muzzle brakes*

Hugh Henriksen Tool, Talent, Oregon 541-535-2309 *Reamers*

JGS Precision Tool, Coos Bay, OR 541-267-4331   www.jgstools.com
Reamers, tooling, etc

MSC Industrial Supply Co   1-800-645-7270 www.mscdirect.com   *Tooling, supplies*

NECO   1-800-451-3550   www.neconos.com   *Slugging bullets*

Pacific Tool and Gauge, White City, OR 97503, 541-826-5808
www.pacifictoolandgauge.com *Reamers, bushings, range rods, etc*

References, cont:

Precision Matthews, Pittsburgh, PA 15205 412-787-2876
www.PrecisionMatthews.com *Gunsmith lathes, mills, etc*

The Viper (Bob Pastor), Gobles, MI 49055   261-521-3671 www.viperbench-rest.com *Viper Chambering Fixture, Viper's Venom cutting oil, etc*

Gordy's Precision / Extreme Accuracy Institute, 913 NE 86th St, Kansas City, MO 64155 (formerly Pella, IA)   641-780-5085
www.GordysPrecision.com   www.ExtremeAccuracyInstitute.com
Custom rifle building and accurizing, instructional DVDs, precision rifle building/gunsmithing classes, 1000 yard/Long range shooting classes, private/one-on-one classes

Special thanks to **Monte McBride** (Kearney, MO) for the great mechanical drawings used in Gordy's part of the book

About the Authors...

Gordy Gritters is a full-time professional gunsmith who has been gunsmithing since 1987. His business was in Pella, Iowa from 1987 until he moved his shop to Kansas City, MO in 2011. He has done a lot of general gunsmithing, repairs, refinishing, and rebluing over the years, but his primary focus all these years has been on accurizing factory rifles and building extremely accurate custom rifles.

Gordy got involved in competitive benchrest shooting soon after beginning his gunsmithing career. He started Iowa's first BR-50 rimfire benchrest range. Then he was instrumental in starting and operating a 200 yard club benchrest match at the Marion County Sportsmans Club range, which is still going strong today. He has been the Rangemaster for all of the Varmint Hunter Jamboree matches in Pierre SD.

Gordy then wanted to get involved in 1000 yard benchrest competition, and since there were no 1000 yard ranges in the Midwest, he founded the Iowa 1000 Yard Benchrest Association in 2002, which held registered IBS 1000 yard benchrest matches until 2010. The Iowa club hosted two IBS 1000 Yard National Championships during this time.

Gordy has built rifles that have set many club, state, national, and world records, and that have won numerous State, Regional and National Championships in a number of disciplines, including 1000 Yard Benchrest and F-Class competition.

Gordy helped Grizzly Industrial design their line of Gunsmith's Lathes, which are designed for chambering high-accuracy rifle barrels. He then worked with Grizzly to produce an instructional

DVD called "Chambering a Championship Match Barrel" to show how to use his chambering techniques.

Gordy was frequently one of the featured speakers at the Varmint Hunter Jamboree symposiums, and has written numerous technical articles that have been published in Varmint Hunter Magazine over the years. He has some of these articles posted on his website under the "Published Articles" tab.

Gordy has been on Varmint Hunter Magazine's "Gunsmith Advisory Panel" since the mid-1990's, and has helped many people over the years with all aspects of their gunsmith training, questions, or problems since then. He has been instrumental in helping a lot of new gunsmiths around the world set up shop and start their own businesses.

Gordy has taught NRA summer gunsmithing classes for three years at Murray State College in Oklahoma. These classes were in precision rifle smithing with an emphasis on accurizing AR-15 type rifles.

Gordy now teaches precision rifle-building and accurizing classes several times a year in his shop in Kansas City, as well as being available for teaching private classes at other shops around the country. All his classes and instructional DVD's are geared toward both do-it-yourselfers and professional gunsmiths.

He is in the process of developing the "Extreme Accuracy Series" of instructional precision gunsmithing DVD's to help others learn the fine art of building and accurizing rifles. These DVD's are available through his website, as well as through other vendors in the US.

Website: www.GordysPrecision.com
www.ExtremeAccuracyInstitute.com

Fred Zeglin has been building custom rifles for over 30 years and specializes in wildcat designs for his clients. He is currently the Firearms Technology Coordinator and the Short Term Gunsmithing Program Coordinator for Flathead Community College in Kalispell, MT. He owns 4D Reamer Rentals Ltd. so he deals with more reamers and headspace gauges than any other gunsmith you will ever meet.

He has taught NRA Gunsmithing courses in Wildcat Cartridge Design at Murray State College in Oklahoma, Flathead Valley Community College in Montana and Trinidad State Junior College in Colorado. Fred also worked with AGI to create a Wildcat Cartridge lesson and Reloading instruction on DVD.

Fred has written articles for Precision Shooting Magazine, Guns and Ammo, and many others. He hosted an award winning podcast about gunsmithing (past episodes are archived) at:
http://www.stitcher.com/podcast/gunsmithing-radio
Fred also writes a gunsmithing blog, that can be found at:
https://gunsmithtalk.wordpress.com

Andy Hill at Hawk Bullets, had this to say about Fred, "During the normal course of business we have gotten to know some gunsmiths with superb skills, artists crafting metal and wood into fine and functional firearms. Usually their ballistic knowledge is well rounded, but we believe one such gunsmith is quickly becoming a modern day P.O. Ackley. He is Fred Zeglin and he has done extensive development of a line of wildcat cartridges gaining popularity for their ballistic properties and low felt recoil." Fine praise from a craftsman of quality bullets.

This book is part of a series of gunsmith manuals that Fred is writing and editing. Titles include: Understanding Headspace, Chambering for Ackley Cartridges, Relining Barrels, Glass Bedding Rifles for Stability and Accuracy, and Chambering Rifle Barrels for Accuracy. Look for other books in the: "Gunsmithing Student Handbook Series".

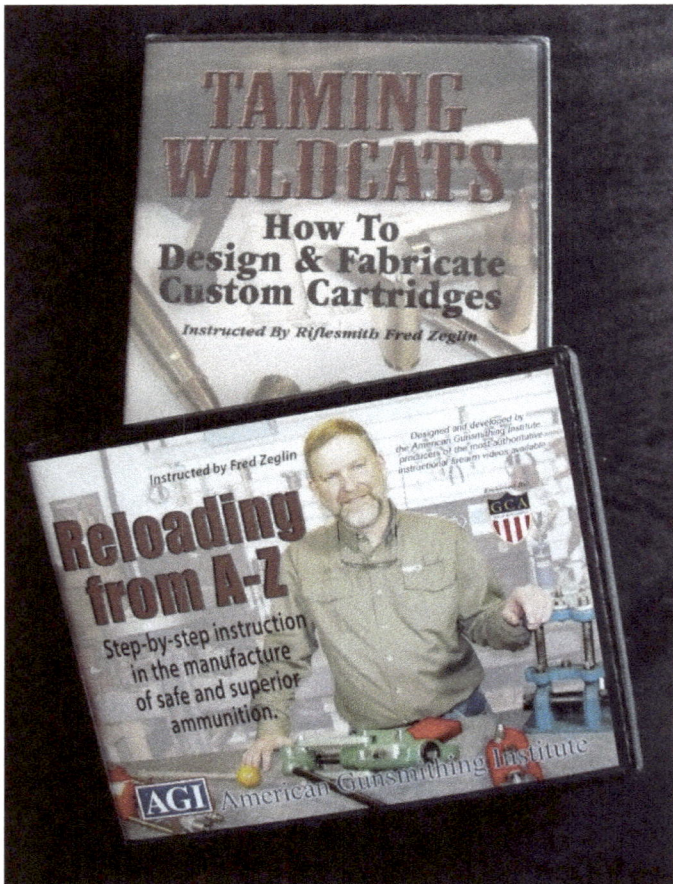

Video Courses Fred has done for AGI.

Hawk Reloading Manual

This hardback book contains 188 pages of stories, illustrations, anecdotes, instructions, and data.

Hawk Cartridges are unusual in wildcat circles in that, correctly headstamped brass is available for them. In partnership with Z-Hat Custom Inc., Quality Cartridge of Hollywood, NJ manufactures the brass.

Each cartridge covered in the book includes a dimensioned drawing. Contributions from Wayne van Zwoll, Michael Petrov, Dick Williams and Mike Brady are included. Pressure tested data is included for the majority of the load data and all loads are real world tested in firearms.

History of Hawk Cartridges is presented. This collection of data includes new material and new cartridges that were not included in the earlier electronic version of the manual. The intention is to provide information that time has shown to be valuable to shooters of Hawk Cartridges and for cartridge collectors. You can buy the Hawk Manual @: http://www.4-dproducts.com/

Can be purchased on Amazon.com
Hawk Reloading Manual

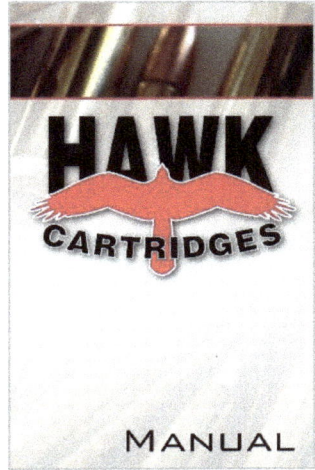

Wildcat Cartridges,
Reloader's Handbook of Wildcat Cartridge Design

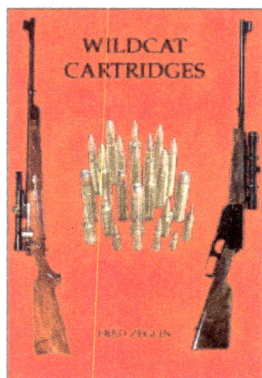

Wildcatting has been around almost as long as the metallic cartridge case. Wildcats have an air of mystery about them, no effort is made in these pages to diminish that mystique. Yet, you will find information here that is simply not available anywhere else. P.O. Ackley was the last Gunsmith to address the subject of wildcatting in depth. Over forty years later, Fred Zeglin, Master Rifle Builder and wildcatter has assembled in an easy to read, often humorous manual for anyone who loves guns, reloading, or wildcat cartridges.

History of wildcat cartridges is presented including many well known designers like P.O. Ackley, Jerry Gebby, and Charles Newton. The historical information provides an appropriate frame of reference for wildcatting. Nobody really wants to repeat something that has already been done. More recent wildcats are included along with reloading data and dimensions wherever possible.

Most valuable of all is the how-to information about making reamers and reloading dies. Fred supplies dimensions and instructions on how they are used to produce highly accurate reloading dies and chambers. Delivery times for such custom tools can delay a wildcat project by many months, knowing how to make your own dies can speed delivery of custom projects considerably.

Can be purchased on Amazon.com
Wildcat Cartridges,
Reloader's Handbook of Wildcat Cartridge Design

P.O. Ackley, America's Gunsmith

Parker Otto Ackley is arguably the most important gunsmith of the 20th century. He trained an incredible number of gunsmiths and shared a wealth of firearms knowledge along the way. The eminent gunsmith, ballistician, barrel maker, teacher and writer perhaps had more influence on modern shooting and firearms than any other single person. And now his life and works have been painstakingly detailed in *P.O. Ackley, America's Gunsmith.*

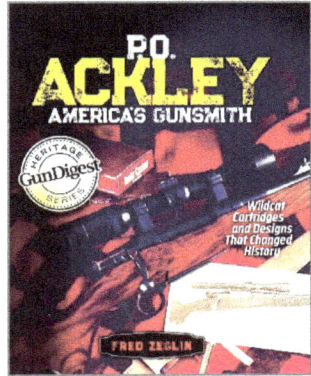

Writer and gunsmith Fred Zeglin gives a never-before-seen look at the humble man whose research thrust the firearms industry forward. From pushing rifle chambers to their limits and developing superior barrels to designing red-hot cartridges, readers will walk away with a new appreciation for Ackley's exploration and ideas. And his concepts on reloading, rifle accuracy, safety, cartridge choice, and wildcat use are just as relevant for today's "gun cranks" as they were in Ackley's heyday.

Zeglin also delivers the most complete collection of accurate dimensions, loading data (much of it with pressure data) and history for the lifetime of cartridges created by P.O. Ackley.

Most shooters today know him because of his "Ackley Improved" cartridge designs. But those cartridges are only the tip of the iceberg. *P.O. Ackley, America's Gunsmith* is the whole story.

Bonus: Full-color photo section and an exclusive never-before-printed article by P.O. Ackley.

You can buy P.O. Ackley, America's Gunsmith @:
http://www.4-dproducts.com

.

www.ingramcontent.com/pod-product-compliance
Lightning Source LLC
Chambersburg PA
CBHW050805270326
41926CB00025B/4553